NOW YOU SEE IT

The Heart of Dyslexia

NOW YOU SEE IT

The Heart of Dyslexia

Karin R. Merkle

Now You See It: The Heart of Dyslexia

Cover design by Paige Litz – Spizzirri Press, Inc.

Photos and illustrations by Karin Merkle unless noted otherwise

Stories, examples, and photographs that make reference or allude to lessons are from one-on-one specialized lessons using the *Barton Reading & Spelling System®*

Faces and names have been used with permission

Written and printed in the United States of America

ISBN-13: 978-0-6921-5292-8
ISBN-10: 069215292X

Dedicated to big-hearted, curious
and crunched-for-time teachers

ACKNOWLEDGEMENTS

Just the right doors closed and opened, to guide me through the perfect combination of people, experiences, and opportunities for this book to become a reality. I acknowledge and am thankful for God's hand in my life as I learn to seek Him first and trust His timing. "For those who wait upon God get fresh strength." - Isaiah 40:29

Thank you, Susan Barton, for giving a free community talk that first opened my eyes to dyslexia. Thank you for creating a user-friendly and immensely successful way to teach reading and spelling.

Thank you, Tammy and Angela, for being the first spark. I never would have guessed that my career would so drastically change its course after our paths crossed and we first uttered the word "dyslexia" as a mere possibility.

Thank you, Tim, Jacey, and Erik, for your support and encouragement. Ludge.

Thank you to my family and friends, for your support and encouragement. I love you.

Thank you to the countless families and individuals I have met along this fascinating and rewarding journey. I continue to learn so much from all of you. You are amazing.

Everybody is a genius. But if you judge a fish by its ability to climb a tree, it will live its whole life believing it is stupid.

-Albert Einstein

The eye sees only what the mind is prepared to comprehend.

-Robertson Davies

Remember Magic Eye® books? Each page looked like a colorful kaleidoscope image. Hidden within each page was a three-dimensional image or scene. For some, the scenes would pop into view quickly and easily. For others, like me at first, seeing the 3-D scene was not an easy task.

Intense staring at a Magic Eye page only brought me eye strain and skepticism: "You're tricking me! There is *no way* that there's a picture of a giraffe on this page!" When much effort was expended to follow the "viewing instructions" and tips from others, I might catch a quick glimpse of the hidden scene. Then I would blink in excitement or move my eyes to take in more of the scene and poof! It was gone.

With frequent practice and experience, seeing the hidden picture becomes easier and easier.

Dyslexia is the "hidden picture". For some, dyslexia pops into view quickly and easily. For others, like me at first, seeing dyslexia was not an easy task, even as an experienced educator.

With frequent practice and experience, seeing dyslexia becomes easier and easier.

The stories and pictures shared with you in this book are from my practice and experience. They are compiled in hopes that dyslexia might be more easily seen and so that more teachers and parents can say, **"Now, I See It."**

Contents

BEFORE DIVING IN

Unless I mention otherwise, the examples, pictures, and stories in this book were observed with my own eyes and ears.

Knowing that teachers are not researchers and their lives are beyond busy, this book is designed to be a quick way to get a taste of dyslexia, without statistics and technical terms. Although I have an understanding of terms like graphemes, Broca's area, parietal lobe, articulation, Wernicke's area, and occipito-temporal area, I defer to the experts and mountains of books, podcasts, videos, and other resources to teach about those terms in detail. I have listed many of those resources in Appendix C for those who would like to learn more.

Dyslexia exhibits a variety of combinations of the characteristics listed in this book as "signs of dyslexia". A student might show a few of the strengths or struggles in this book and *not* have dyslexia. Alternatively, a student *with dyslexia* will not show each and every one of the strengths or struggles in this book. For example, many of my students reverse letters when they read or write, but not all of them do. Many of my students have poor handwriting, and yet the handwriting of other students is beautiful. Some are late to talk and get tongue tied often, but others might not have any issues in the area of speech.

The examples in this book represent what dyslexia looks like in both boys and girls and in people of all ages.

This book will not cover all there is to know about dyslexia and won't cover all the possible signs of it. My purpose is to give a quick glimpse into dyslexia for parents and for teachers who were not taught about it in their teacher preparation courses. For the first fifteen years of my teaching career, I did not understand nor recognize dyslexia.

I am still learning. It's not as a researcher or expert but as a fellow educator, fascinated and impassioned by dyslexia, that I share my learning and experiences.

Ideally, this book will plant a seed that leads to instructional changes. In the meantime, the purpose of this book is to change the way parents and teachers view struggling readers and to open their eyes to these students' strengths, creativity, and potential.

NOT TO BLAME

I can't wait to show you what dyslexia looks like, so I was tempted to skip this section and head right to the "Dyslexia IS" part. But I hear so many cringe-worthy statements about dyslexia that are just not true. I felt the need to address them here, first.

<u>Heard from teachers, parents, and the general public:</u>

"She's not trying hard enough."

"It can't be dyslexia since he doesn't reverse b's and d's."

"He needs to apply himself."

"If only her parents would have read to her when she was younger."

"He'll grow out of it."

"She's so smart. She will catch on."

"He needs to repeat a grade."

"Dyslexia doesn't exist."

"He just doesn't *want* to read. He'll do fine once we find a book that interests him."

"She's too young. Let's wait and see."

"He needs to slow down."

"She is just not paying attention."

"Your child can't have dyslexia because she's getting A's and B's."

"Dyslexia means you can't read."

"He just needs to spend more time practicing reading."

"I've never had a student with dyslexia."

"He knew how to read that word yesterday."

"Reading and spelling struggles happen because the English language is so crazy."

"She is not low enough to qualify for any help."

"Dyslexia is seeing backwards, right?"

"My child got dyslexia back in 3rd grade when he was sick and missed a lot of school."

"She's just not as smart as my other kids."

"He's just lazy."

"I think she got dyslexia in 2nd grade when she had an inexperienced teacher."

"Do you teach them to read the other way?" someone asked, while pointing right to left.

"I think we just didn't read enough over the summer."

"My child can't have dyslexia because she is very smart.

DYSLEXIA IS

Dyslexia is genetic and neurological in nature. It is a language processing difference in the brain that can make spelling, reading, speech and writing more difficult, despite intelligence and motivation.

Dyslexia is not caused by a bad year in school or by anything parents do or don't do. The "brain wiring" that comes with dyslexia exists at birth. Dyslexia occurs in the rich and in the poor. It occurs to both boys and girls. Dyslexia occurs in people with low intelligence and in those with high intelligence. It occurs in students with little parental support and in those with heavy parental support. It occurs to those who have had no exposure to books and to those who are surrounded by books and have been read to since birth. Dyslexia exists in people of all ages and all languages.

Kids who struggle to read are likely bright, talented kids who just need to be taught reading and spelling differently than how schools typically teach it.

An area exists in the brain that handles reading and spelling tasks efficiently and makes language tasks seem automatic. In the brains of people with dyslexia, the "wires" just aren't going to that language area. So even though people with dyslexia *can read*, the part of the brain that handles language most effectively is not being utilized. Instead, different areas of their brains are activated to try to help with language tasks. This uses much more energy and brain power, so tasks like reading or writing are laborious and exhausting. For more information about the language center of the brain, images of the brain/dyslexia, and the neural signature of dyslexia, see ***Dr. Sally Shaywitz, Ben Foss***, and ***Dr. Stanislas Dehaene*** in Appendix C.

Dyslexia is biological, so although it might appear to "show up" in 3rd or 4th grade, it was actually there all along. Dyslexia only begins to rear its head when strategies that worked for the student in the past stop being effective (often in 3rd or 4th grade).

Students do not know that they have been using ineffective or inefficient techniques like memorization, repetition, and relying on context or picture clues. They think *everyone* reads and spells this way, so when language tasks become difficult, they often start to believe that something is wrong with them and that they must be stupid.

STRENGTHS

A quick online search reveals high numbers of intelligent, innovative, creative adults with dyslexia. Digging a little deeper, there are common similarities found in what they remember of their past:

Cold sweats and a feeling of dread at the thought of having to read out loud.

Fear of looking stupid.

Fear that they actually *were* stupid.

Being sent to special classes for reading.

Having a hard time with reading and spelling.

Labeled as "slow learners" or "lazy".

Others telling them that they would not amount to much in life.

I will say right up front that not every kid with dyslexia will turn into a Steve Jobs or an Agatha Christie. But I wonder how much society has missed out on, based on the incorrect assumption that poor reading and spelling ability must somehow mean less intelligence or less potential in life.

People with dyslexia are a treasure to our society. Sometimes, a little digging is needed to find it. Other times, it takes shape and shines through early on. It is vitally important to recognize and help develop the strengths in people with dyslexia, otherwise the treasure might remain buried and hidden. Undiscovered treasure increases the chances that a person will end up on the wrong path.

Juvenile delinquency programs and jails are full of people with dyslexia. But, the realms of entrepreneurs, business leaders and successful adults in all careers are *also* full of people with dyslexia.

Dyslexia is accompanied by a number of strengths like excellent thinking skills, ability to figure things out, curiosity, great imagination, talent at building, athletics, superb people skills, music, art, design, and engineering, to name a few.

Mechanical skill is also common. My students love to fix things. I often hear, "He can't read or spell worth a darn, but he can take anything apart and put it back together!" or "I don't know how she did it but she fixed the _____!"

For many, the strength is in areas of science and math; their logic and problem-solving skills are incredible and they often find solutions that no one else would have thought of.

Although they might struggle at reading a book, many are incredible at reading *people*. They carefully observe the tiniest of actions, facial expressions, and body language. They are kind, intuitive and sensitive to the needs of others and can be deeply empathetic.

Creativity and the natural ability to visualize a finished product before it is constructed are common skills. Legos®, Minecraft®, wooden blocks, K'Nex®, and Nanoblocks® are some well-known building materials, but I've seen students make things out of popsicle sticks, cardboard, duct tape, and scraps of any kind.

Those with effective and expressive communication skills make good leaders, pastors, teachers, and presenters. They listen, communicate, act, and speak in public with natural skill and flair.

People with dyslexia do not all share the same strengths. Drawing, for example, is a strength that a few of my students have. They amaze me with their sketches and designs. Most of my students, however, avoid drawing altogether since their attempts turn out to be shaky stick-figure scratches that do not look AT ALL like the image they are trying to represent. The sample of drawing and writing below is from a 5th grader. He was so flabbergasted that I didn't recognize the drawing as "E.T." that he wrote, "How do you not get this?" This very same student, though, excelled in hockey. His room was covered in trophies and medals galore that he had received in recognition of his star hockey skills.

Hockey, BMX, basketball, competitive swim, rodeo, and dance are just a few of the athletic areas in which my students excel. The number of medals, 1st place awards, and trophies (some as tall as a person!) that they have earned is incredible!

But athletics isn't a strength for all my students. In fact, some are clumsy and awkward in anything that relates to physical activity.

If a student can survive the school years with encouragement from teachers or parents, "You may not be a very good speller, but wow, look how good you are at _____ and _____!" then his/her chances of success in the "real world" are likely.

People with dyslexia are not always able to recognize their own strengths or may not be aware that their abilities are unique or unusually good.

- "I thought *everyone* could picture the inner workings and gears of a motor or machine." – Dale, Electrician

- One student could not name ONE strength of his, even after much prompting from me. Turns out he has a bunch of strengths, including archery, academics (he made the honor roll after getting structured literacy instruction), a great sense of humor, creativity, and robotics, to name a few! He plans to go to an engineering college and I have no doubt that he will.

- One student thought her pictures for photography class "were the same as everyone else's" until her teacher pulled her aside and told her, "You really have an eye for what makes a good photo."

The possibilities for strengths really are unlimited and many of the categories I have listed will overlap, but the following pages will give you some examples.

CLEVER – ENTERTAINING – WITTY – HUMOROUS – FUN TO BE AROUND:
♥ While learning that -ture says "cher", this clever student decided to have some fun. Check out his spelling of the word "chirp":

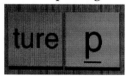

♥ To suit their values or to be silly, students have been known to change or add words in the sentences or stories we read. For example, the phrase "hit the puppy" was changed by several students to read, "hug/love/pet the puppy" and "Bill did not tell his boss he was ill," became "Bill did not tell his boss he was BATMAN." One student added the word "Please" to the beginning of a command he was spelling (Bring me a glass of rosé while I sauté the mushrooms), "so it didn't sound so demanding."

♥ This student used the *at* symbol (@), when spelling the word "Atlantic":

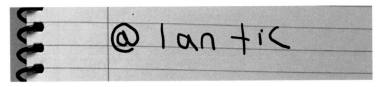

♥ When learning that certain combinations of letters look like a closed syllable (in which the vowel makes its short sound) but don't *act* like a closed syllable like -old/sold and -ild/wild, a student created a text-like message for me out of wooden tiles:

All in good fun, I had a reply for him:

♥ Well, the directions *did* say, "Put a <u>box</u> around the 3 letters at the end."

 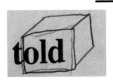 

♥ Early lessons show the value of learning to read and spell nonsense words. Accurate spelling or reading of a nonsense word reveals whether or not students understand and can apply a recently-taught rule. In addition, nonsense words can exist as parts of longer words. For example, *fac* could be considered a nonsense word or it might be the first syllable of words like *factory* or *factual*. *Nav* could be a nonsense word or it might be the first syllable of a real word like *navigation*. After reading the nonsense word *fas*, my student thought of some real words that started with *fas*, like *faster*, *fasten*, and *fascinating*. After reading the nonsense word *bap*, I asked, "Can you think of any longer words that start with *bap*?" With no words coming to her mind, my student replied, "Baaaaaaaaaaaaaap."

♥ I hear interesting takes all the time, such as, "I have so many memories in my head that if you walked into my brain that would be the first thing you ran into," and "Knuckles are just like mini knees!"

♥ One day during a remote session on my computer, I grabbed my mouse and moved to close one computer window to go to a new part of the lesson. I became panicked when I could not find the "X" that needed to be clicked on in the upper right-hand corner in order to close the window. Where had it gone? I couldn't close the window, there was no scroll option, and I couldn't even minimize the window. After several seconds of desperate searching and bewilderment, my student began to chuckle. Turns out he had used the annotate tools of Zoom to discreetly put a small black rectangle shape over all the icons in the upper right of my screen, including the X!

When I call my students "nerds" or "stinkers" I say it with a laugh and I mean it in the most loving of ways.

TALENT AT ARCHITECTURE AND PATTERNS:

Students' natural ability to build and create is evident even when I first meet them. Although not at all scientific nor part of any real screening, I've found it fun and fascinating to observe how students react when I place fifteen blank colored tiles in front of them. I do eventually use the wooden tiles to check students' ability to sequence, discriminate between sounds and to represent words, syllables, and sounds. But BEFORE that, I tell them, "We will be using these tiles in a minute, just as soon as I get this form ready," and then I turn my eyes to a recording sheet and pretend to be busy filling it out.

It really only takes me a few seconds to write a name and date on the top of the form and then I am secretly but intently watching in anticipation to see what the student does with the tiles.

Rather than waiting with their hands in their lap, students with dyslexia tend to be drawn immediately to the tiles. It's as if the tiles were magnets, pulling the students' hands in and begging to be stacked, sorted by color, or made into a design or structure.

Without any direction or examples to follow, students transform the tiles into patterns, towers, walls, domino-lines, tunnels, stairs, pyramids (some flat, some standing up on end). Given the choice to wait for me for ten seconds or to create, the students inevitably create.

Partially due to trying to look busy "getting the form ready" but also because I found students' creations interesting, I started using the top corner of the form to jot a few quick observations in the margin of my recording sheet (see picture, below). I've typed a sampling of them below the picture, for easier reading.

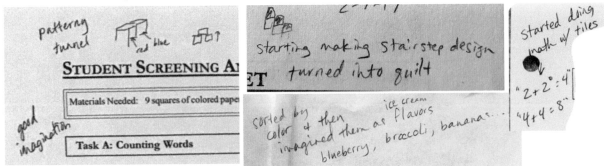

The student…

- built a staircase, then sorted by color, then stacked into a tower by color.
- first made pattern in a line, from left to right: blue, red, green, yellow, orange, blue, red. Then made a symmetrical "robot".
- started making stairstep design then turned it into a "quilt".
- started doing math with the tiles: "2 + 2 = 4", "4 + 4 = 8".
- noticed right away, "There's three of every color!" He then began counting the tiles by color in multiples of three: "3…6…9…12…", then placed stacks of tiles between the fingers of his palm-down hand.
- built a wall, symmetrical in design and color, then built "a king's table."
- made a symmetrical design with all the tiles rotated into diamonds.
- counted tiles, then stacked them into tower, then built a symmetrical design and wall.
- sorted (the tiles) by color and then imagined each color-pile as flavors, "Blueberry… broccoli… bananas…"
- made a horizontal line, added tiles on both ends, equally and simultaneously, then built a pyramid.
- imagined the yellow tiles as "Mini pads of sticky notes!"

- created multiples "flags", then pointed to the green and yellow one and cheered, "Go Packers!"

The student...

- stacked tiles into a tower, formed a rectangle, counted the tiles, then sorted the tiles into columns by color, in the order of colors in a rainbow.

- immediately sorted by color and made same-shaped piles.

- built different configurations of rectangles (3 x 5, 2 x 6, 3 x 4...).

Here are a few other amazing designs:

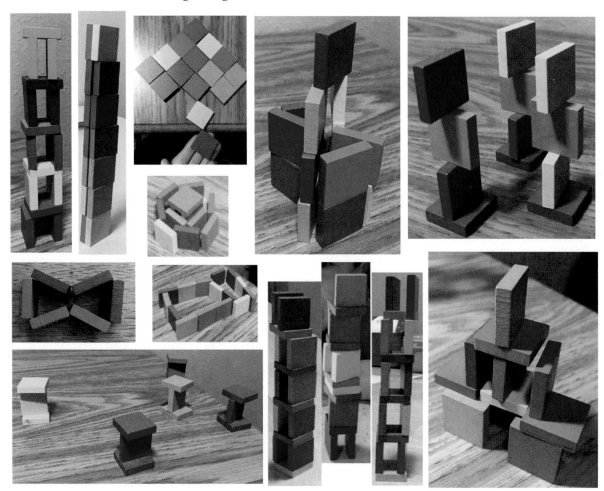

♥ One girl showed geometric understanding and skill by first showing a small square of four tiles. Then she showed how to proportionally enlarge the square by adding five tiles all at once, along two edges of the little square, in the shape of a V. For a video of this creation, see "Little Square/Big Square" in Appendix A.

♥ The following two designs were created by girls. I only point this out to highlight the fact that dyslexia AND engineering skills happen just as frequently in girls as boys! Since the first picture was blurry, I tried to recreate the tile design to take a better picture, but changed my mind when building it was harder than it looked! Both designs took careful balancing and engineering.

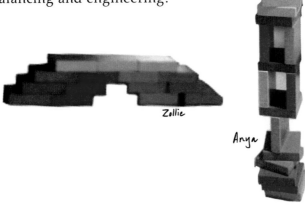

Zollie

Anya

♥ One time, I accidentally brought out an incomplete set of tiles. Normally numbering three of each color (red, green, blue, yellow, orange), one green tile was missing. Neither the student nor I noticed that the green tile was missing, at first. After watching them moving purposefully and swiftly for several seconds, the student's hands suddenly became still. The student sat there, staring and the gears in his head turning, as he tried to figure out how to complete his design. A combination of politeness and shyness prevented him from alerting me about the missing tile. I finally noticed his discomfort and the imbalance of his design and quickly went to my office to find another green tile. When I put the tile in his hand, the student seemed relieved. He immediately placed the green tile into its spot in a now perfectly symmetrical pyramid.

PATTERN-FINDERS – ULTIMATE NOTICERS:

Although my students may not notice the differences between similar-looking *words* (like split/spilt and mouth/month) or similar-looking *letters* (like h and n), they notice the teeniest of details of everything else. They will notice details in the background of story book pictures and differences between the same model of car ("I could tell that wasn't your Subaru because the rims are different."). They are the first to perceive a new arrangement of items on a shelf, a haircut, new glasses, or subtle body language. They make something from "nothing" by finding shapes, patterns or designs in their student sheets or surroundings.

♥ In the student practice sheets that require connecting words across two columns, many students notice a pattern, design, or shape in the criss-crossed lines. I'm not sure to which one he was referring, but in the example below, the student pointed out the "capital A".

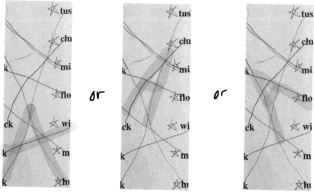

♥ "There's a kid in my class who is known to struggle academically, but he seems to find patterns in numbers that the rest of the students don't see." – Gena, Learning Coach

♥ After using an eraser to make a spelling change on his paper, a student brushed the eraser shavings into the margin, where he noticed that the eraser shavings seemed to have arranged themselves in the shape of a face. He proceeded to sketch over the eraser shavings what he perceived as the eyes, then the nose, then the eyebrows of the image until he had drawn the whole face. I captured a picture of his drawing (below), but unfortunately only after he had brushed aside the eraser shavings:

♥ In reviewing a few prefixes, I typed them onto an online whiteboard for a student. After typing the prefixes (below) for her, she asked pointedly, "Did you do that on purpose?!" I had no idea what she was talking about until she pointed out that I had made a pyramid/pattern: two letters, then three, then four, then five.

u p
m i d
o v e r
i n t e r

♥ "What?" I asked a student who appeared to be staring up past his practice sheet. Still staring, he replied, "The design in the wood looks like the bird on your coffee mug."

<u>ART – DESIGN:</u>

Although I don't have photo evidence of all my students' amazing creations and art, including photography, sculpture, drawing, design, painting, fashion, and crafts, here are a few examples of some pieces of art and quick margin doodles:

The following sketches and doodles are all from one student artist, T.B:

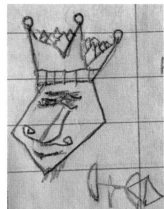

This fellow's eyes started out as the student's written reminder that the vowel team eu can say either "yoo" or "oo".

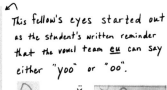

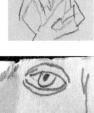

on the lawn)

IMAGINATIVE – INNOVATIVE – EFFICIENT – ENTREPRENEURIAL:

♥ One student shared what he enjoys: "I like to let all my energy out at recess. I run around with my imagination and like to pretend I'm in the world of Minecraft."

♥ My students and I make use of an iPad with digital letter tiles during our lessons. For one of the spelling portions, students use the digital tiles to spell words. When a student has finished spelling a word, I ask the student to read the word to check it and then I press a button that erases the whole work area on the screen and proceed to say the next word to be spelled. More than one student has figured out that if a tile or word part in the existing word is needed in the next word, the student can put his finger on those tiles before hitting the erase button. In doing this, all the tiles will erase except for the ones the student is touching.

♥ After reading a one-page story about the North Star and thinking about how many stars there are, one student analogized, "Imagine our body as a galaxy. The cells are like stars."

Students sometimes share goals/dreams for the future. Some that I've heard include the following:

- Inventing
- Being a scientist
- Owning a company
- Creating a new, living thing
- Building and running an elaborate ice cream parlor/factory
- Building a dragster
- Being able to fly
- Seeing the moon up close
- Being a designer
- Buying an island
- Being a doctor
- Going into nanotechnology
- Becoming an astrophysicist

♥ An innovative young man showed me his hand-made "goat chute" that he used for roping practice. He had rigged it up with a bungee cord and hooks so that at the pull of a rope, the front wooden door would not only unlatch, but would spring open quickly. For the link to a video, in which he demonstrates it, see Appendix A.

CRITICAL THINKERS – INQUISITIVE – ASK "WHY?" and "WHAT IF?", and "HOW?":

♥ A 7-year-old drew my attention to the digital letter tiles on the screen of my iPad (exact replicas of the real-life wooden tiles) and asked, "Can these tiles be turned?" I figured he was just investigating the digital tricks and figuring out if he could rotate them. When I answered, "No," he thought carefully and then asked, "Then why does there need to be a line on the bottom of the b, d, and p?"

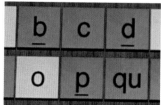

♥ After asking a student to repeat back a silly sentence about a wild animal eating spaghetti (likely designed to check pronunciation of longer words) a 7-year-old student admonished, "Animals eat meat or plants!"

♥ After learning the prefix *semi* (meaning *part* or *half*) and then reading the word *semicircle*, a student wondered aloud if there were such a thing as a semisquare. We decided together that a semisquare would be a rectangle or a triangle, depending on how a square was halved.

Students usually have good comprehension and critical thinking skills when a story is read TO them or when they learn to decode/read for themselves. They are reflective, logical, and insightful.

During specialized reading lessons, each word of the sentences and stories is deliberately chosen in order to keep the vocabulary controlled (students are only given words to read that they have been taught how to decode). Because of this, and to give extra practice with a newly-taught type of syllable or reading rule, the wording sometimes ends up a little wonky. I am pleased when students read the phrases and sentences accurately, but I am even more pleased to see that they are thinking critically about what they read.

♥ After reading a sentence about a woman wearing bifocals and listening to the radio, a student asked, "Why does she need bifocals to listen to music?"

♥ After reading about a buffalo chewing oats, a student corrected, "A buffalo doesn't eat oats. It eats grass!"

♥ After reading a sentence about a gold nugget being worth trillions of dollars, a student responded, "That must have been quite the discovery. I don't think anyone in the world is actually a trillionaire."

♥ After reading about a boy who stepped on a frog and fell into an icy pond, a student asked, "Why would there be a frog out there in the winter?"

KNOWLEDGEABLE – INTELLIGENT:

Reading and spelling struggles can easily mask a student's intelligence. I personally know amazing medical doctors, lawyers, and engineers with dyslexia. Knowing that intelligence and knowledge are common characteristics of dyslexia makes it easier to look past reading and writing mistakes of young students and imagine their potential.

♥ Before I even knew about dyslexia, a 2nd grader in one of my reading groups displayed both the struggles and the strengths of dyslexia. He had a hard time when it came to reading, but he was clearly very intelligent and knowledgeable. He was articulate and used good vocabulary. He could identify any kind of dinosaur (even the ones with complicated names) and he could tell you anything and everything about them.

♥ I asked a student to help me think of a way to more easily remember that the Greek word-form *tetra* means "four" (for other students, but also for ME!). Right away, he suggested the game *Tetris®* but then immediately dismissed the idea, embarrassed and thinking he was way off base. With further consideration, we made the realization that in the game *Tetris®*, the shapes that fall from the top are all just different configurations of FOUR squares! According to dictionary.net, the name Tetris is a combination of the Greek prefix *tetra* (meaning four) and *tennis*, the game designer's favorite sport. That was a connection I never would have made and now I have a way to remember that tetra means four!

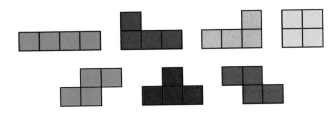

♥ One student could not read the word *lost* when I first met him, but psychological testing from around that same time showed his IQ level at "Superior".

♥ One year, a student and I met at a coffee shop for early morning lessons. Twice a week, we would enjoy black coffee over a lesson and then I would drive him over to his high school just in time for his first period class. His vocabulary and knowledge shone through in our conversation in the short car ride to his school. There was talk of new innovations, the science news of the day, and the student's dreams for the future, which usually involved an invention of some sort and owning his own island someday.

One day, the topic turned to some features of the new Tesla®. He spoke with ease about the difference between hydrophilic and hydrophobic vehicle seats. His clear explanation of *hydrophilic* versus *hydrophobic* prompted a vocabulary realization of my own and I excitedly shared with him that we would soon learn the following Greek word forms in our lessons:

hydro = water   **phil = fond of**   **phobe = fear of**

Knowing the meaning of those Greek word parts, can you, the reader, tell which of the two seats (hydrophilic and hydrophobic) repelled water and which one soaked in the water and became wet?

Once students have unlocked the code and logic of language through specialized lessons, academic honors are likely. I get frequent emails or pictures from proud parents or happy students telling me good news like the following:

- Students are more independent with homework.

- Students' grades on the report card have gone up.

- Students have made the Honor Roll.

- Students have graduated with Honors

- Students have taken state standardized tests and scored "proficient" or "advanced".

- Students have scored at or above grade-level on achievement tests.

- Students have earned high SAT or ACT scores.

♥ The California Achievement Test (CAT) scores from this 4th grader, Anya (on the following page), flipped the narrative that she was "a slow learner, had trouble staying on task, and was not reading enough." Having already been held back a grade in school, she went from feeling frustrated, overwhelmed and always behind, to being an avid reader and wowing with her scores after three main changes:

1. She found out that she had dyslexia, just like her dad (a doctorate level engineer) and she excels in math and science, just like her dad.

2. She received phonemic awareness training followed by explicit, systematic phonics instruction.

3. Her mom decided to homeschool her, where she could listen to audiobooks, go at her own pace, and have accommodations such as verbal testing and extra time.

Items to note on the CAT scores:

- It was <u>not</u> <u>timed</u> (many students know the information being tested, but simply run out of time to complete the test).
- Her highest grade-equivalent score came in Reading Comprehension.
- All of her scores were above grade-level (She was in 4th grade at the time).

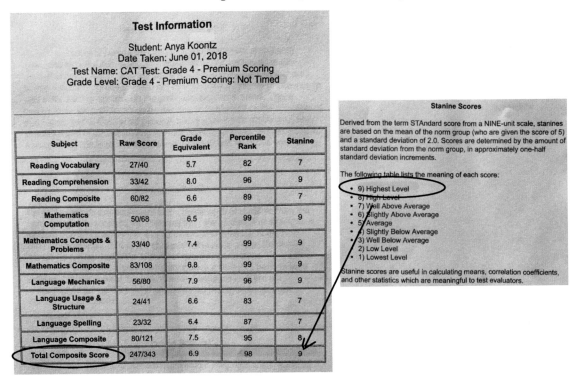

Test Information

Student: Anya Koontz
Date Taken: June 01, 2018
Test Name: CAT Test: Grade 4 - Premium Scoring
Grade Level: Grade 4 - Premium Scoring: Not Timed

Subject	Raw Score	Grade Equivalent	Percentile Rank	Stanine
Reading Vocabulary	27/40	5.7	82	7
Reading Comprehension	33/42	8.0	96	9
Reading Composite	60/82	6.6	89	7
Mathematics Computation	50/68	6.5	99	9
Mathematics Concepts & Problems	33/40	7.4	99	9
Mathematics Composite	83/108	6.8	99	9
Language Mechanics	56/80	7.9	96	9
Language Usage & Structure	24/41	6.6	83	7
Language Spelling	23/32	6.4	87	7
Language Composite	80/121	7.5	95	8
Total Composite Score	247/343	6.9	98	9

Stanine Scores

Derived from the term STAndard score from a NINE-unit scale, stanines are based on the mean of the norm group (who are given the score of 5) and a standard deviation of 2.0. Scores are determined by the amount of standard deviation from the norm group, in approximately one-half standard deviation increments.

The following table lists the meaning of each score:
- 9) Highest Level
- 8) High Level
- 7) Well Above Average
- 6) Slightly Above Average
- 5) Average
- 4) Slightly Below Average
- 3) Well Below Average
- 2) Low Level
- 1) Lowest Level

Stanine scores are useful in calculating means, correlation coefficients, and other statistics which are meaningful to test evaluators.

✳ Fun update: I just saw Anya the other day at a local ice cream shop, where her grandma bragged to me on how many books she now devours (3 or 4!) per week. With a sly smile, Anya nodded in agreement and then opened the little bag hanging from her shoulder to reveal its contents, a book.

♥ Here are end-of-year Iowa Test scores from an 8th grade student of a fellow structured literacy teacher, before and after he began lessons:

Vocabulary	Pre-8.4	Now-12.8
Rdg. Comp	Pre-5.6	Now-13+
Rdg. Tot	Pre-7.0	Now- 13+
Spelling	Pre-5.3	Now - 7.8
Caps	Pre-5.6	Now- 13+
Punc	Pre-5.0	Now- 12.4
Usage/Exp	Pre-7.5	Now-13+
Lang Tot	Pre-5.7	Now-12.4
Math Tot	Pre 5.8	Now- 13+

♥ Even before seeing their good grades or test scores, I am immensely proud of my students, but getting texts like this is super fun and makes me do a happy dance:

ENGINEERING:

♥ The Dyslexic Advantage organization offers a yearly scholarship opportunity to college students with dyslexia. One of this year's twenty-five recipients, a mechanical engineer student at South Dakota School of Mines and Technology, responded to my congratulatory email by expressing his surprise at how many of the other recipients (all with dyslexia) were also majoring in engineering: "I was so surprised that I got the scholarship. It was fun to read the other stories. I was shocked to see how many of them were engineers." – J.S., Mechanical Engineer student and Private Math Tutor

♥ "In elementary school, I was in the top math classes and the bottom reading classes. It was my 6th grade math teacher that convinced my parents to mainstream me out of resource classes and back into the top classes to match my mathematics skills. The teachers in the honors classes were special. To them, reading was a means to an end, not the end-goal. They saved my future. I am the product of several great understanding teachers, even though none of them knew what dyslexia was. They took the mismatch in reading and writing with science, math, computer science, and engineering in stride. They could see beyond those limitations and help expand my mind through thought." - C.T., Ph.D. Electrical & Computer Engineering, focus in Controls, Applied Math, Physics

♥ "I can see the world much differently than the people who work for me." – Darren, Chemical Engineer

♥ "It is powerful once you understand the amazing way dyslexics think. When I have new products around the house and I'm stuck, I just hand it over to [my son] and he figures it out and gives it back to me and it's done." – Russ, Dad of an Amazing Dyslexic

IMAGINATIVE STORY-TELLERS – HIGH-LEVEL VOCABULARY:

The act of writing words onto a page may be a chore, but dyslexics like Walt Disney, Steven Spielberg, and Patricia Polacco show that vivid imagination and the ability to tell a story can be tremendous strengths for people with dyslexia. To read more about these storytellers, see Appendix C.

♥ One student I taught in Reading Recovery was very smart and super creative. Her classroom teacher once shared an eight-page story the 1st grade girl had written. The story was full of reversals and spelling errors but it was also full of imagination, expression, fantastic word-choice, and personality.

Students who have learned information in ways other than reading text (like being read to, involvement in new things, conversation, audiobooks, documentaries, history shows, science videos, and hands-on activities), often show their intelligence and good learning ability through their use of spoken word and conversation.

♥ "The Dropping Rule" reminds students that if a word ends with a silent e (like the word *care*), the silent e must be dropped before adding a suffix that starts with a vowel (like *-ing*, or *-ed*). One student wanted to call this rule "The **Plummeting** Rule".

♥ After reading the phrase, *"the glass window"* and once again after the phrase, *"a jobless bum"*, a 3rd grade student commented, "Well that's redundant!"

♥ When taking the post-test for one of the structured literacy levels we had completed together, a student was being asked to give examples of words to show his understanding of different prefixes. When asked to name a word that used the prefix *inter*, meaning "between two or more things", words like *interstate*, *internet*, and *interact* would have been perfectly acceptable. For *his* example, my student decided upon "intersocietal cooperation".

A quick online search of "dyslexia" and any area of strength will produce a good list of famous or successful people with dyslexia who excel at what they do and who can be good role models for students. Seeing other successful people with dyslexia can help make students realize that they are not alone and can help them see their own potential.

To learn more about the strengths that accompany dyslexia and for the names of some people and organizations that focus on the strengths of dyslexia, see Appendix C.

REVERSALS/TRANSPOSITIONS

Just like in the strengths section, you'll find overlap and recurring themes in the stories and observations ahead. The most overlapping trait is with the often-misunderstood but most well-known trait associated with dyslexia: **reversals**.

The switching of the way a letter or number is facing (left/right or up/down), the changing around of the order of letters or numbers, or the swapping of sounds, syllables, or whole words all constitute a reversal of sorts, so reversals might be better named "transpositions". According to dictionary.com, **transpose** means "to change the relative position, order, or sequence of; cause to change places; interchange".

Although reversals and transpositions are often blamed on "seeing things backwards" or "letters jumping around on the page", transpositions are not caused by vision. One piece of evidence for this is that even transposition of SOUNDS is a common occurrence.

Transpositions in SOUNDS (no text, just verbal):

Given the spoken sounds (ĕ), (n), and (d) (no written letters, just sounds) to blend together to make the word "end", the student said, "Ned" (same sounds, different sequence).

Given the spoken sounds (k), (p), (k) (no written letters) just to repeat back to me, many students have said the right sounds, but in this order: (p), (k), (p).

I spoke the nonsense spoken word, "BIP" (no written letters), and asked a student to repeat it, say it slowly, and then break apart and identify the individual sounds within in it. The student correctly repeated the word, stretched it out "/b   iiiiiii   p/" but then named the individual sounds in this order: (p), (i), (b).

One student had recently taken an SRI (Scholastic Reading Inventory) test, she excitedly told me that since last time, her "IRS score" had gone up considerably.

A student told me of his lunch at "Har_b_ees". He meant *Har_d_ees*.

With dyslexia, transpositions can actually be observed in ALL the areas of language: spelling, writing, reading and even speech!

Transpositions in SPELLING

Transposition of sounds can result in spelling errors. While learning about silent e, I spoke the word "take" for a student to spell. The student correctly repeated the word "take" and then wrote **kate**. Other examples:

fan tuskit (fantastic)   alwayy (always)   ni to (into)

Transpositions in SPEECH:

Many mispronunciations are just a "reversal" of sounds. Immediately after I said the word, "token" for a student to repeat (and then spell). He repeated back, "ko-ten". Other examples:

Yew Nork   aminal   baksetball   stain tration

Transpositions in DIRECTION, TIME, and SPACE:

Trouble with terms like "before" and "after" or "first" and "last"
Confusion with terms like "yesterday" and "tomorrow" or "earlier" and "later"
Difficulty reading clocks with hands
Hard time using maps
Constantly confuses "left" and "right"
Trouble with directions like "north, south, east, and west"
May even confuse "up" and "down" or "forward" and "backward"

Transpositions in WRITING:

1-4-19 (4-1)   jumg (jump)   mild (wild) / minter (winter)   fig (fig)

Transpositions in READING:

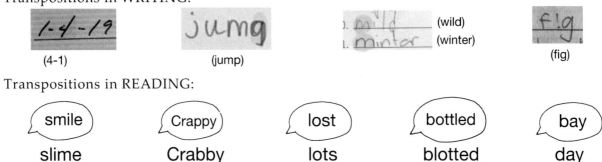

smile / slime   Crappy / Crabby   lost / lots   bottled / blotted   bay / day

Transpositions are not caused by an issue with vision or the eyes (with the switching of SOUNDS as proof). Rather, the reversals, flips, and switches are due to a non-linear way of thinking, a 3D perception skill, a lack of phonemic awareness, and a processing difference *in the brain*.

Non-linear

People with dyslexia have great strength in seeing "the big picture" of a story, problem, or situation. While this is helpful when problem-solving, imagining, understanding, and creating, it can be troublesome when dealing with tasks that require linear thinking. The word *linear* means "related to a line". It refers to steps that need to be followed in a specific order or a certain direction.

Putting together a puzzle, sketching or painting an image, and getting a look at a long-lost friend, building a car, looking at an object = not linear.

Steps in reading, spelling, typing, texting, solving many math problems, efficient handwriting, and tying shoe laces = linear.

Since many people with dyslexia do not naturally think in a linear way, tasks with a specific sequence of steps that need to be followed in order or in a certain direction like left to right, can be difficult, especially without explicit training and practice.

The following examples show how sequences can get scrambled before a brain is trained to process linearly:

Given a sequence of three spoken sounds (no written letters, just sounds) to repeat back, students sometimes repeat back the sounds out of sequence:

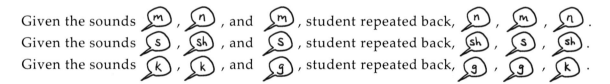

Students are given the spoken sounds i, p, and s (no written letters, just sounds), to blend together. Successful sequencing and blending of those three sounds would result in the nonsense word "ips". On more than a few occasions, students correctly repeat the three individual sounds, but then somewhere between hearing the individual sounds and saying the sounds blended together into a word, the sequencing gets out of order and the student says, "isp" or "sip".

I have given the sounds sh, i, and f, expecting the nonsense word "shif". The student correctly repeated the sounds, in the correct sequence, but then said, "fish".

Presented with a sheet of words or math problems, students sometimes read the words in random order, start with a problem in the second column or halfway down the page, and skip around in no particular order.

♥ One young man was taking the vision test for his driver's license. When he started reading off the letters, everyone was confused and ready to blame a vision problem until they figured out that the boy was naming the items on the chart in random order, as his eyes fell on them. A similar experience was shared by another family, who had taken their daughter for an eye appointment. They became concerned about her vision when it appeared that she could not see the letters. Turns out she was just skipping around on the eye chart, naming the items in no particular order.

♥ When presented with the word *cabin*, a student might start with "/b/" or "/n/" (sound).

♥ I've been told by an adult with dyslexia that she reads by taking in a whole page at a time, looking at random spots on the page and being able to get "the gist" of the passage.

Eye experts might claim that a young reader's struggles are due to a tracking problem (inability to move eyes smoothly from left to right, word to word on a page) and that vision therapy is needed to correct the eyes from jumping around on a page, but it is not uncommon for students' eyes to do this before they break the code of reading and begin attending to the structure of the words from left to right. In other words, before students learn how to track and read linearly, they tend to skip around on a page in order to gather as much information as they can to piece together what the story or reading passage might be about.

♥ One mom reported that her daughter once read the word *to* as "ot", and I observed the girl read the vowel-team *oy* as "yo".

I have to remind students, "You are very good at visualizing images and that helps you construct amazing things. But when forming the letter d, you have to start here with your pencil and then go this way," or "You are very good at seeing the big picture and that helps you to solve problems. But with reading, you have to start here with your eyes and then go this way."

Even with students in the upper levels of structured literacy instruction, I occasionally need to point to the first letter of a word and say "Start here."

♥ Just today, a bright student had to be reminded that the order of the letters matters in reading. A normally accurate and fluent reader, he said "Waston" instead of *Watson* and "dasmel" instead of *damsel*. Since both those words were new to him, he needed prompting to return to them and try them again, this time slowing down to note the order of the letters (and therefore the order in which to say the sounds).

3D Perception

People with dyslexia have strength with imagining and working with things that are three-dimensional (3D).

Since students appear to have a good grasp of three-dimensional objects, I believe that until they are taught differently, they try to use that strength to help them with flat, two-dimensional things like letters and words on a page.

♥ Imagine people lining both sides of a street and watching a parade. Many of the floats have large helium balloons attached. When a balloon of Superman goes by, then watchers on both sides of the street will recognize the balloon as Superman. When a balloon of the letter d goes by, then even though people on both sides of the street are looking at the same balloon, one side of the street sees the balloon as a "b" and the other side of the street sees the balloon as a "d". If letters/words/shapes are treated like 3 dimensional objects (like a balloon) rather than 2 dimensional (like on paper), the letter/word could qualify as different things, depending upon the perception of the viewer.

It's not that people with dyslexia *see* symbols any differently than everyone else. Their eyes see the same exact shape. But imagining a flat letter or word as 3D object and without knowing from which direction to perceive and process it, the person has to just take a stab at it. Sometimes the guess is correct and sometimes it's not.

Below are other examples where confusion is due to perception and viewpoint. None of the examples involve dyslexia, but are designed to show why some tasks like reading, writing, looking at a clock with hands, reading a map, distinguishing between "before" or "after", writing the letter b or d, using greater than or less than symbols (> <) can be tricky for people with dyslexia.

♥ Imagine going to a child's or grandchild's concert or play and wanting to know where she will be standing so you can get a seat with the best view of her. She tells you, "I'm on the left side of the risers." You walk in and find a seat on the left, only to find out that the child meant **her** left, as she's standing on the stage.

♥ After being called for jury duty, I was mailed a parking pass to put in the windshield of my car. The directions clearly stated to "Place the parking pass in the lower right-hand side" of the windshield. I struggled to know whether that meant the lower right as I was sitting in my car or the lower right as I was outside and looking at my car. I had to just make a guess.

♥ I'm notorious for being uncoordinated when it comes to learning a new dance routine or exercise motions. I think it's worse for me if the instructor (in person or on screen) is facing me. I just don't know if I am to mirror the instructor (if she raises her right hand, I should raise my left hand) or if I should copy her motions (if she raises her right hand, I should raise my right hand). And since the routine goes by too fast for me to think it through, I end up kicking when I should be punching and I end up turning left when I should turn right.

If it is hard to imagine the connection between the examples and dyslexia, try thinking of a transparent sheet or a window with something written on it. If a person is not sure from which side to "read" the message, it would be challenging. Take this image of a waving guy painted on the glass door of a store as an example: 🧑 On your way *in*, you would think that he was looking at you and waving **hello** with his right hand. On your way *out* of the store ten minutes later, you approach the same exact image, but from the back: 🧑 Now you view him as looking at you and waving **goodbye** with his left hand. Neither painting is "backwards" and yet the image sends a different message depending on how it's viewed.

Examples of 3D Skill:
♥ A student called me over to see the design he had built from flat geometrical math tiles (shown below). "Three cubes," was all he said. It was a neat design, but I struggled and struggled to see why he called it "three cubes". Mickey Mouse, maybe. Princess Leia, maybe, but "three cubes"?

"Three Cubes"

It took me a few minutes of concentrating, but then an amazing thing happened. The 3D cubes popped into view. It took my brain a long time to perceive what my student's brain easily saw. Once I did see the design as 3D, it was hard for me to notice the flat hexagon. My experience with this student's design is the reason for the yellow hexagon on the book's cover. ☺ If you can't see the three cubes in his design, then see a hint and/or find the link to a short video of the design in Appendix A. For some fun "What-do-YOU-see?" activities related to this, see Appendix B.

♥ After correctly reading the word *cubic* on a page from her reading lesson, a 2nd grade student inquired as to what the word cubic meant. I explained that to measure something flat, like from point A to point B on the floor, I would use a ruler. To measure something *not* flat, like the space in whole room (I gestured width, length, and height with my hands), I would need to measure in cubes, giving me *cubic* feet. The student showed instant understanding and began to visualize as she looked up to the corner of the room. "Yes, so if I put a cube up there, and then another one there..." Her voice trailed off as she imagined one cube after another and then determined, "This room would fit a lot of cubes!"

In addition to perceiving flat images as 3D, the untrained brain doesn't really pay attention to the orientation/direction of an image or object. No matter the direction this truck is facing, and no matter where your eyes first land on the image, you will recognize it as a truck.

It's not just for people with dyslexia that object direction is unimportant. In fact, the way a 3D object is facing doesn't matter that much to *anyone*, until the need to decipher printed text arises.

According to Dr. Stanislas Dehaene a cognitive neuroscientist, everyone is born with somewhat of a "symmetry generalization" in their brain. This generalization allows people to recognize objects and faces no matter their orientation in space. For more information about mirror-images and symmetry generalization, see **Stanislas Dehaene**, Appendix C.

Since everyone's brain has this symmetry feature at first, it is not uncommon to see mirror writing and letter reversals in the early years of school, **even in children who do not have dyslexia.**

Donavan

Shania

Reading scientists, fMRI scans, reading specialists, and neuroscientists all tell us that when a child learns to read by attending to the structure of the word (letters and words in order, from top to bottom and from left to right) then the brain physically changes. The brain learns to treat letters differently than objects, the language center of the brain becomes more active, the symmetry generalization feature is "unlearned" for written language, and the reversals go away.

When reversals in reading and writing continue into the second and third years of school and beyond, then it becomes a huge clue that the child **has dyslexia** or the child's brain **has not learned <u>how</u> to read**, or both. The child may appear to be reading, but is likely treating words as 3D objects, thereby using memorization and guessing, rather than by attending to the letters and parts of a word in a linear way. This causes slow, choppy, and inaccurate reading. And reversals.

♥ One of the oddest things relayed to me by a colleague was of a 1ˢᵗ grader she observed. When the young girl encountered an unknown word, she would move her index finger to the end of the word and begin to curl her index finger. She did this often. Although we will never know for sure, I would venture a guess that the girl was trying to turn the word or lift it up, as if getting a good look at all sides of the word might help.

I once found myself behind a Jeep with a spare tire cover with a picture of the head of a deer with on it. The picture below is not very clear, so I'll try to explain what I saw. Under the deer, I saw the Jeep name, but upside down. Since I recognized the Jeep lettering, my brain saw it as "Jeep", but upside down. My first thought was that someone had put the tire cover on upside down. Then I thought it might be one of those "I've been off-roading. If this is upside down, get help" jokes. But the picture of the deer was right side up. Strange.

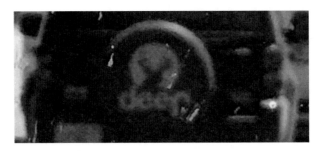

The problem was that my mind recognized the whole shape as "Jeep" and would have thought "Jeep" no matter which way it was facing. When I processed the upside-down Jeep lettering from left to right, though, I finally figured out that when upside down, the "p" in Jeep became the first letter of the word and represented a "d". The letter "J" (upside-down) represented the *last* letter: a fairly elongated, disproportional lowercase "r". The word was a little trick on the brain and not actually *Jeep*, but *deer*. Online, under "Jeep deer tire cover" there are images of the ee's right side up and upside down. Either way, my mind reads it as "Jeep", but upside down.

♥ While still teaching in a public school and working one-on-one with 1st graders, I was trained to ask questions designed to help evaluate a student's "print awareness". I would show the page of a book with some sort of print error (often missing punctuation, misuse of capital letters, or transposed letters, words, or lines) and then ask, "What's wrong with this?"

On one occasion, before meeting one of my students, I painstakingly wrote the following sentence on a whiteboard:

When I asked her the standard, "What's wrong with this?" she first read the sentence perfectly, "Sally ran to play." She then stated that the word *play* needed to be below the word *Sally*, "otherwise it would be 'play. Sally ran to'." There was never a mention that the whole sentence was ***upside-down***.

Even saying, "Look carefully," or "See if you can find the error," students are hard-pressed to notice transpositions.

♥ One mom pointed out to her daughter that she had written the number 5 backwards on her math paper. The girl laughed it off as a silly mistake, then erased a *correctly* formed 5 on the worksheet and rewrote it backwards.

Even telling students, "The round part of the letter **d** always goes to your left," or "Form a **b** just like in your name," is not helpful. Although you would think that exposure and practice would solve the problem, many students will reverse or transpose letters in their own names.

Before students are taught to treat letters, numbers, and words differently than 3D objects, they simply ***do not notice*** rotated, flipped, or reversed images as being backwards.

For other fun perception and processing illusions and thought-provoking ideas, see "Can a star be backwards?" in Appendix B.

Phonemic Awareness

Having phonemic (fo-NEE-mic) awareness is not about hearing, necessarily, but means being *aware* that spoken words are made up of small individual sounds (phonemes) and that sounds can be added, removed, changed, or rearranged to make new words. In order to be a good reader and speller, a person must have phonemic awareness.

Since this section includes references to sounds, slash marks around a letter or letters indicate the *sound* represented by that letter or letters. For example, /k/ means the *sound* that you hear at the beginning of words like *kitten* and *caterpillar*. The sound /k/ can be spelled by the letters, C, CK, and K. In Greek words, /k/ is spelled with the letters CH, as in *chemistry*.

A phoneme (pronounced FO-neem) is the smallest unit of spoken sound in our language.

A knock on a door and a hand clap are both sounds, but to count as a phoneme, a sound must be part of a spoken word.

Since a phoneme is a sound, eyes cannot see it. Therefore, a written letter is not a phoneme. Also, a letter name is not a phoneme. The sound at the beginning of the word *"bear"* is not "B" ("bee"), but /b/. In fact, in order to say most letter names, several phonemes are needed. To say the letter "X" by its name actually takes three phonemes: "/e/.../k/.../s/". To say the letter "C" by its name takes two phonemes: "/s/.../ee/".

Since NO LETTERS are involved, phonemic awareness activities can be done in the dark.

Most words have more than one phoneme, all smooshed together. For example, if I say the three phonemes /f/.../i/.../sh/, blended together in that order, I will say, "fish".

The word *sawed* and the word *sod* have the exact same three phonemes: /s/.../o/.../d/.

The word *wrecks* and the word *Rex* have the exact same four phonemes: /r/.../eh/.../k/.../s/.

The word *itch* is four letters and only two phonemes: /ih/.../ch/.

The word *eight* is five letters and only two phonemes: /ay/.../t/.

The word *kit* and the word *kite* both have three phonemes (but the middle one is different).

A group of phonemes can be arranged in different sequences to make different words. An example of this is the word *"felt"*. When I say the word slowly, I can hear that it has four phonemes: /f/.../e/.../l/.../t/. When I change the order of those exact phonemes, I end up with a different word: /l/.../e/.../f/.../t/ = *"left"*. The phonemes in the word *"came"* (/k/.../ay/.../m/) said backwards become *"make"*.

The word *"may"* is spelled with three letters, but it only has two phonemes: /m/.../ay/. If I say those same phonemes in a different order and say /ay/ first, then I say, "/ay/.../m/" and end up with the word "aim".

In trying to think of another good example of rearranged phonemes, I hit the jackpot! As I tried different sequences of the phonemes in the word *task,* I was excited to discover that the same four phonemes could be rearranged to make **eleven** different words!

The word *task* has four phonemes: /t/ /a/ /s/ /k/.

1. /t/ /a/ /s/ /k/- - - blended in this order makes the word TASK

2. /t/ /a/ /k/ /s/- - - blended in this order makes the word TACKS

3. /t/ /a/ /k/ /s/- - - blended in this order makes the word TAX

4. /a/ /k/ /t/ /s/- - - blended in this order makes the word ACTS

5. /k/ /a/ /s/ /t/- - - blended in this order makes the word CAST

6. /a/ /k/ /s/ /t/- - - blended in this order makes the word AXED

7. /k/ /a/ /t/ /s/- - - blended in this order makes the word CATS

8. /s/ /k/ /a/ /t/- - - blended in this order makes the word SCAT

9. /s/ /t/ /a/ /k/- - - blended in this order makes the word STACK

10. /s/ /a/ /k/ /t/- - - blended in this order makes the word SACKED

11. /a/ /s/ /k/ /t/- - - blended in this order makes the word ASKED

Without phonemic awareness, even when kids are taught letter sounds, spelling rules, or "sounding out" (blending the letter sounds together to make a word), it may not make sense or stick. Without phonemic awareness, students are missing an important foundation and will not advance into skilled, efficient reading.

Here are a few real examples of students trying to read a word, using basic phonics and sounding out, but without phonemic awareness:

"/m/.../a/.../t/......rug."

"/h/.../a/.../t/......mittens."

"/m/.../u/.../s/.../t/......saved?"

"/B/.../e/.../n/......Tom."

Being able to visualize a picture of a word or its letters does not equate to having phonemic awareness. Some students can appear to have phonemic awareness by passing some basic tasks like being able to produce words that rhyme or by picturing and manipulating letters in their head rather than actually being aware of the sounds/phonemes. Here are some clues that give it away:

♥ One student was clearly picturing letters rather than sounds of a word when I asked, "What *sound* do you hear at the end of the word, *path*?" Rather than giving me the /th/ sound, the girl first said "H" (as in the letter's name) and then changed to a sound, "/h/", as though that was the answer I was looking for.

♥ Another student, when asked the first sound in *chop* responded "C", rather than /ch/.

♥ One student answered "/y/" (like *yes*) to "What *sound* do you hear at the end of the word, *baby*?", likely picturing the letter Y and then translating it to its consonant sound.

♥ Me: "What is the first sound you hear in the word *van*?"
   Student: "V" (letter name)
   Me: "Okay, what *sound* is that?"
   Student: "I don't know."

Many student's develop awareness of the sounds of our language, starting with whole words and syllables and then moving to the smallest pieces of sound, through oral language, read-alouds, nursery rhymes, and songs. I absolutely encourage those types of activities, but for students who do not pick up an awareness of phonemes despite those activities, phonemic awareness can be taught.

Students must have seven different phonemic awareness skills in order to become good readers and spellers. For information on those seven phonemic awareness skills, see *Susan Barton*, in Appendix C. For information about the importance of phonemic awareness proficiency and a program for advanced phonemic awareness, see *Dr. David Kilpatrick* in Appendix C.

Brain Processing

In understanding the language struggles of dyslexia (areas of reading, writing, spelling, and speech), <u>sound</u> is key. Accurate reading and spelling hinges upon sounds and how well the brain processes those sounds.

Think of language processing as:

1. **the taking in** of information into the brain, whether through the eyes, ears, or fingers
2. a taking apart and putting back together of that information while keeping it in the same sequence
3. and then **the spitting out** of that information, whether through the mouth or fingers.

No matter the language task, sound is involved in the processing at some point or another:

- In the act of <u>reading</u>, even though the eyes are needed to see text, it is the brain's job to process that visual information by translating the code on the page into <u>sound</u> (even if the person is reading silently).

- In the act of <u>writing and spelling</u>, even though the ears are needed to hear words, it is the brain's job to process that auditory information by being aware of the individual <u>sounds</u> within spoken words, translating those sounds into symbols, and then recording the correct sequence of those sounds/symbols onto paper.

- In the act of <u>speech</u>, even though the mouth, tongue, and vocal cords are needed to speak words, it is the brain's job to process information by recalling words and processing the <u>sounds</u> of those words so they will come out of the mouth in the correct order.

Simply put, how well the brain processes **sound** determines the ease or difficulty of tasks like reading, writing, spelling, and speech.

In the next several sections, you'll see examples of dyslexia. In other words, you'll see what happens in spelling, writing, reading, and speech when a perfectly smart brain does not think linearly, is unsure how to perceive written text, or has difficulty processing sounds.

SPELLING

What dyslexia looks like in spelling:

- spending time and energy to learn a list of words for the classroom spelling test, only to forget how to spell the words a few weeks later

- poor spelling, even by people with great intelligence

- right letters, wrong order

- starts and ends the same as the intended word, or shaped similarly

- reversals and transpositions

- poor spelling, even on common words and irregular words that have been used over and over

- missing part of a blend (bl, nd) or digraph (th, sh, ch)

- little or no knowledge of phonics (like how to spell /k/, when to double letters, and reasons for a silent e)

- confusing similar sounds, like /s/ and /z/ or /v/ and /f/

Poor spelling ability is one of the best indicators of dyslexia.

Although visual memory is very helpful in learning to spell words, it is not reliable as the main or only way to learn to spell. Accurate spelling relies on the ability to hear the sounds in words, in the order that they are spoken, and then knowing which letter or letters to use to spell/represent those sounds.

Some people possess an awareness of those sounds early on and their brains pick up on the spelling patterns of our language without instruction, so they end up being good spellers without much effort. Others need to be taught how to pay attention to the sounds in spoken words and then need to be explicitly and systematically taught the structure and spelling rules of words in our language.

Without an awareness of the sounds within words and without knowing the "hows and whys" of spelling, students are left with trying to memorize random strings of letters or memorizing whole words visually. Techniques to memorize the spelling of a word might include saying its letters repeatedly, writing the word on paper over and over, using memory tricks, word activities and games, and being quizzed by mom and dad (especially the morning before a spelling test!). Trying to memorize the spelling of a word might work for a little while, but there are just too many words in our language for this to be effective and reliable.

When I ask parents about their child's spelling, they often say, "Well, her spelling is pretty good. She has an A in spelling." For a true reflection of a student's spelling ability, check daily assignments, writing, written notes, or a spontaneous piece of writing with no editing. Or, wait a few weeks after the class spelling test was given and dictate the same words for the student to spell.

Time and energy to memorize spelling:

♥ A concerned mom gave me her daughter's school pretest results (shown below). I'm usually pretty good at deciphering "dyslexic spelling", but I can only guess a few of these. That means she is *not even close* to getting these words correct. Which means she had to try to learn (memorize) the beginnings, middles, and ends of every single word. Without knowing the logic behind why the words are spelled the way they are, learning these words in time for Friday's spelling test is much like trying to memorize a list of phone numbers or a list of random passwords.

Spelling pretest 3   9/8/14

1. lefu
2. bet
3. esey
4. jens
5. step
6. rele
7. mena
8. egre
9. rechu
10. quna
11. sped
12. stret
13. pleas
14. bresu
15. reser
16. drevs
17. clend
18. betwen
19. sede
20. sesu
21. breth
22. proskr

I witnessed a few young students who could correctly spell a word, but had absolutely no knowledge of letters or the word's connection to sounds. It was like the word was **drawn**, like a picture. For example, a 1st grade student could correctly write out his name, but could not answer any questions about the details of his name.

ME: How many letters in your name?   STUDENT: I don't know.
ME: What is this letter (pointing to the p)?   STUDENT: I don't know.
ME: What is the first letter of your name?   STUDENT: I don't know.
ME: What is the first sound in your name?   STUDENT: I don't know.

♥ One young student knew that the word *mom* was, "Two Ms with an O in the middle!" but rather than write it from left to right, he drew the two Ms (each from right to left) and then added an O in the middle. To him, he could just have easily been drawing an object, like a flower.

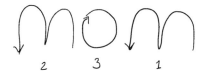

♥ After writing her last name, one student apologized for **the letter _n_** by saying, "I'm not very good at a lowercase h."

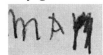

♥ A literacy teacher approached me, wondering how in the world she could get a student of hers to spell the word *at*. She lamented, "I have told her over and over, "'A...T...*at* A...T...*at* A...T...*at* A...T...*at'*, but she still doesn't remember." This story could just as easily be told about learning to **read** the word *at*.

There are definitely some words that have an irregular spelling (like *does* and *said*) and need to be memorized, but by and large, neither spelling nor reading is about remembering.

In fact, you can tell when a student has not been taught the connection between the sounds in spoken words (phonemes) and the symbols written to represent those sounds (graphemes/letters) when a student looks up, as if searching for a visual picture of the word and then says something like, "I'm trying to remember how to spell *with*." or "I used to know how to spell *went*."

Some people treat *every* word as though it needs to be visually remembered. Even though kids see the word *stop* all the time, young students will usually spell it SOP (all capitals like the sign) or SOTP. They try to picture a stop sign rather than record the letters that represent the sounds in the order that they are heard.

The following examples show what happens when people, even teenagers and adults, try to spell a word by relying on their memory of a word's appearance.

♥ In the image below, you'll see that someone wrote the word *prescription* at the top of a paper, and even helpfully divided it into syllables for a student to practice spelling. Unfortunately, this ended up being an exercise in copying, which is a difficult task for students with dyslexia. At the beginning of the activity, the student copied the slash marks that were there to divide the word into syllables. At some point, the slash mark morphed into the letter 'y'. Soon, the slash mark is reversed and then dropped completely. Other letters were dropped or changed along the way, and eventually the student's 'r' becomes a 't'. Despite the hard work and time spent, the student misspelled the word *prescription* on her classroom spelling test:

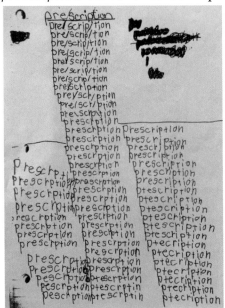

♥ There have been two different instances in which students have spelled *apple* starting with the letters *Aa* and one boy spelled the name *Austin* starting with *Aa*. I have a hunch that all were a result of seeing *Aa* along with a picture of an apple on the alphabet strip hung up along the top of every primary classroom wall.

One student: _____Aappl_____

Another student: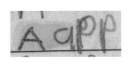

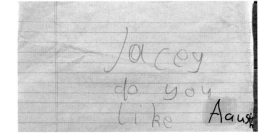

Right letters, wrong order:

While gathering and sorting examples of students' attempts at spelling the sentence, "The quick brown fox jumped over the lazy dogs," I found many examples of students spelling the word *brown* with all the correct letters, but in a completely different order. This is a direct result of learning to spell by visual memory and exposure, rather than learning to say a word slowly and write a symbol (letter or letters) for each sound heard, in the order that it was heard. Although there is one vowel-team (ow) in the word *brown*, the rest of the sounds are represented simply, by a single letter: "/b/ = **b**, /r/ = **r**, /ow/ = **ow**, /n/ = **n**."

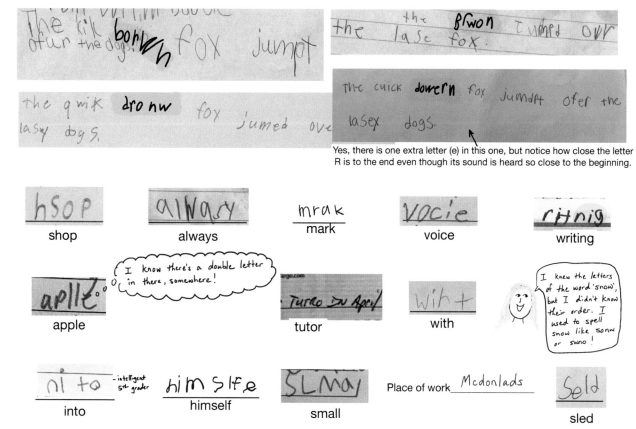

Yes, there is one extra letter (e) in this one, but notice how close the letter R is to the end even though its sound is heard so close to the beginning.

Missing part of a blend or digraph:

A **blend** is two or three consonant sounds/letters, in a row, like the SPL in *splash* or the letters BL and ND in the word *blend*.

A **digraph** is two letters that make just one sound, like CK, CH, TH, and SH. A digraph can be found in a blend, as in the letters NCH at the end of the word *bench* or the letters SHR at the beginning of the word *shriek*.

41

Reversals / Transpositions:

Sometimes, a letter's incorrect orientation may be transposed due to the reasons described in the" Reversals/Transposition" section. Other times a flipped letter may be due to sound confusion. For example, a student spelling *crobs* for the word *crops* might have up/down confusion or might confuse the <u>b</u> sound with the <u>p</u> sound since they are actually very similar.

- **Left/Right errors** are errors in which a letter is "flipped" to the right or to the left, like the page of a book. Common examples of this include the letters b/d, p/q, and s/z.

- **Up/Down errors** are errors in which a letter is "flipped" up or down, like a light switch. Common examples of this include the letters b/p, u/n, and w/m. For a video of up/down confusion, see Appendix A.

pounds   bank   captain   moment

apple   month   done   strong

map   plant   table   republic

shop   dogs   pounds   shop

bring   done / said / could   cat   drive

hypnosis   box   winter   apple

Lack of knowledge about the logic and structure of our language:

Phonics has been given a bad rap for being "drill and kill" (referring to overdoing practice with worksheets rather than through reading) and for lacking language richness with sentences like "*Jan sat on a log.*" Phonics at its most basic level can seem simple: "If you hear /b/, it is spelled with the letter b," but phonics is more than just letters and their most common sound. I like to think of phonics as "the logic of our language". When phonics is explicitly and systematically taught from simple to advanced, it leads to an understanding of how words work so that stories with rich and complex language can be decoded.

This section contains examples of when a student does not understand the structure and rules of our language.

For example, CK *is* a possible spelling for the /k/ sound, as in *chi<u>ck</u>en* and *tra<u>ck</u>*, but never at the beginning of a word as in the photo below.

crops

The letter T *is* a possible spelling for the /t/ sound, as in *<u>t</u>ime*, *doc<u>t</u>or*, and *fac<u>t</u>*, but not when a person is trying to show past tense, as in *jumped*.

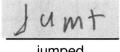
jumped

The suffix -ED *is* a possible spelling for the /d/ sound, as in *tim<u>ed</u>*, *groom<u>ed</u>*, and *follow<u>ed</u>*, but only when a person is trying to show past tense.

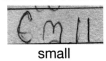
blind   wild

The symbol C *can* be used to represent the sound for /s/, as in *<u>c</u>ity* and *<u>c</u>entennial*, but never before a consonant like the letter M as in the photo below, spelled by a 5th grader.

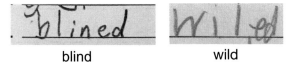
small

Confusion about silent e:

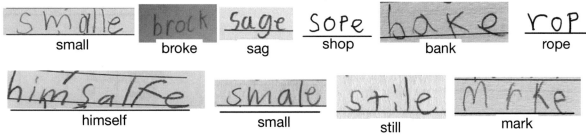
small   broke   sag   shop   bank   rope

himself   small   still   mark

There are pretty basic rules to use in order to spell words like the ones below, but if you don't know the rules, then it becomes a guessing game or a memory test.

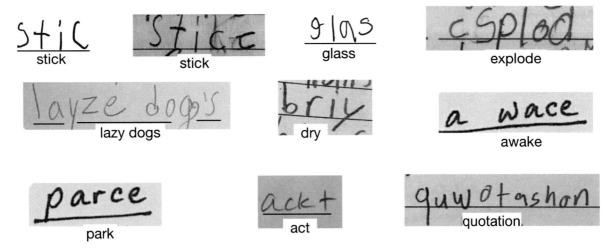

stick

stick

glass

explode

lazy dogs

dry

awake

park

act

quotation

Sound/letter confusion or speech issues

Certain sounds in our language either sound very similar, like /f/-/th/ and /m/-/n/ or are made using the same lip and tongue movements so they look and feel the same. One kid almost didn't believe me when I slowly pronounced the words **truck** and **trick**. He thought the words were "chruck" and "chrick". You'll understand why once you whisper the /tr/ sound and the /chr/ sound one right after the other. They look, sound, and feel very similar. Same with sounds like:

/v/ and /f/
/b/ and /p/
/s/ and /z/
/ch/ and /sh/ and /j/
/t/ and /d/
/k/ and /g/

Also, it's difficult to correctly spell a word when you can't pronounce it (a student who pronounced the word *believe* as "bleve", spelled it that way). Here is how one girl spelled the word *another*:

There is overlap in the categories that follow. For example, one student first wrote the letter 'p' when starting to spell the word **dry**. Another wrote 'tapol' for the word **table**. Both examples could be due to up/down confusion or they could be due to sound confusion since /b/ and /p/ are similar sounds (try whispering those sounds to see for yourself that the lip motions feel and look the same). Errors of m/n confusion, which are highly represented below, could be due to the fact that /m/ and /n/ are similar-sounds or they could be due to the fact that the letters m and n are visually similar.

The following spelling errors could be due to similar-sounding sounds, similar-looking letters, or directionality confusion:

grim / grin	chin / shin	wish / which
Septenber / September	valcon / falcon	maf / math
fibrate / vibrate	japionship / championship	bolf / both

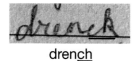
drench

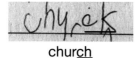
church

quick

trampoline

they

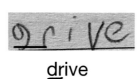
drench

/dr/ and /jr/ (sometimes spelled with a gr) = common confusion

drive

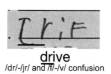
drive

drive

/dr/-/jr/ and /f/-/v/ confusion

drive

lazy

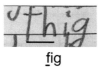
fig

move

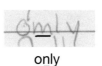
only

table

multible
multiple

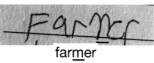
farmer

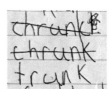

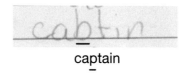
captain

mountain

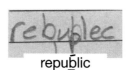
republic

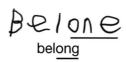
belong

clump

monine
morning

small

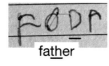
father

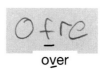
over

move

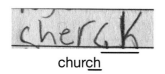
church

unpire
umpire

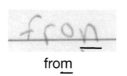
from

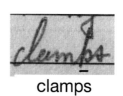
clamps

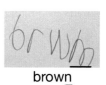
brown

Beginning readers who have not been taught phonemic awareness may try to make a connection to a letter's **name** and the **sound** it makes within words. I think students often rely on what is consistent with most consonants: the initial sound of the letter's name is the same as the sound that it represents within words. For example, the letter D, pronounced "dee" does usually represent /d/ and the letter Z, pronounced "zee" does represent /z/, but that is not the case for many letters. When I check letter/sound correspondence as part of an initial screening and ask, "What sound does this letter make?" here are some responses I've heard from 5ᵗʰ graders, 6ᵗʰ graders, 17-year-olds, and even adults:

- Since the letter C's name is pronounced "<u>s</u>ee", some students think its most common sound is /s/.

- Since the letter G's name is pronounced "<u>j</u>ee", some students think its most common sound is /j/.

- Since the letter W's name is pronounced "<u>d</u>ouble-yoo", some students think it represents the sound /d/.

- Since the letter U's name is pronounced "<u>y</u>oo", some students think it represents the sound /y/ like *yes*.

- Since the letter Y's name is pronounced "<u>w</u>y", some students think it represents the sound /w/.

- Since the letters QU are pronounced "<u>k</u>yoo", some students think they represent the sound /k/ or /kyoo/ like *cu-pid* and *cu-tie*.

- Even though not as common, since the letter X is pronounced, "<u>e</u>ks", I have heard students think it represents /eh/ (like *effort*) rather than /ks/

To make matters worse, the letter C **can** represent /s/ and the letter G **can** represent /j/, and students sometimes think it can go the other way around: since C can say /s/, they think the letter S should be able to say /k/ and since G can say /j/, they think the letter J should also be able to say /g/ (as in *go* and *get*).

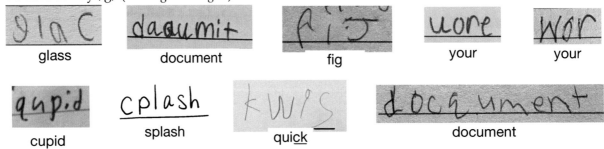

glass   document   fig   your   your

cupid   splash   qui<u>ck</u>   document

Another common mistake is for students to think that the letter Y only represents /y/, as in the words *yes* and *yo-yo* (like the alphabet strip teaches). They may not know that the letter Y represents a vowel sound when it is in the middle or end of a word, as in /ih/ as in the word *typical*, /eye/ as in the words *type* and *my*, and /ee/ as in *candy*.

my   lazy   story   only   dry

I told a 3ʳᵈ-grader named Brycen, "Listen, you have the /eye/ *sound* in your name. /BRI/-/sen/," but because of the Y in his name, he shook his head and insisted that his name had /y/ (consonant sound, like *yes*) in it.

Lots of erasures and crossed out words:

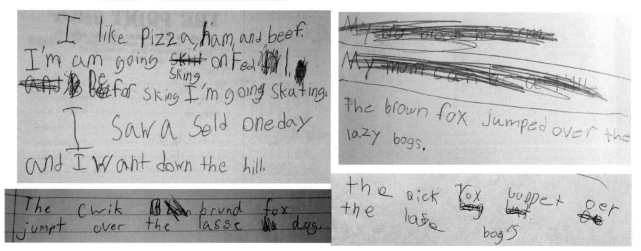

More general examples of what spelling looks like in dyslexia:

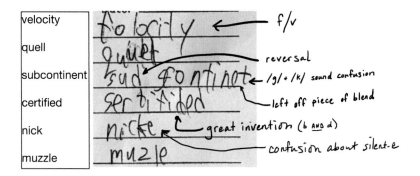

velocity	fo locity	← f/v
quell	Quuel	reversal
subcontinent	sud fontinot	/g/ + /k/ sound confusion
certified	sertified	left off piece of blend
nick	nicke	great invention (b AND d)
muzzle	muzle	confusion about silent-e

The quick brown fox…

The following pages include writing and spelling samples, in which you will see all of the error-types I've mentioned, and more. Some samples are of the student's choosing, some are from a spelling task from the WIST (Word Identification and Spelling Test) and some are students' attempts at spelling a sentence that I have dictated to them. My friend and dyslexia advocate, Jim Huff, had the idea to have students write a sentence as a handwriting sample. Thanks goes to him since I have adopted that idea in my screenings, as well. I took his idea and began using the sentence, "The quick brown fox jumped over the lazy dogs," since it includes at least one instance of every single letter in our alphabet. The sentence-writing task gives good information on pencil grip, hand dominance, letter formation, and *spelling*.

The Quit brwonfox Jumped the lase dog,

The cwic browne fox jompte ovr the lasiy dogs.

$ the quit BAK fox the Jup ovrc lase DOG

the qwik bram baes jumpt over the lasey gdgs

the qwik bram baes jumpt over the lasey gdgs

the kwek bron fox Jompt ovr the lase dog

The caic bran fox jupt ovr the lasy dogs

the auic Beon fox tompt ovr the Lase Dog

the Kee Bon Fots [ot Ofr theLACE DOG

The Quit bron fox Jumed OVER The Lazy dog

The cuic brawne fox Jompt ouver the lase dogs

The QUWik Bawne Fox jumg over the Lasey dogs

the KWIS brwhn fot [ut ovr the lose dogs

The KWiK draon fox Jannt Ofha Lase bogs

the Cwick bromfox Jup over the las bogs

The Cwic brana fox Jumpd ovru the Dog

the kwic brone fox jopde over the lazy bogs

The cit Ban Ex jupt ofr th lase dogs

The Ki Bon fox guqx ovr the Laye Dogs.

the qwick Brawn fox Lompt
ofre the lase bogs

The kvi byn Fax gump over
The 19se bags

the aink bron fox gumt
over the lase bogs

the qeek brone fox jumgedover
the quick brown fox jumped over
the lasy bogs
the lazy dogs.

The Qik brawn
fox jume over
the lasey dog.

the cloc Dog JumptuvrIthe lase Dog Joptuvrothe
brain - brown
fosck - fox

The kwik
brown fox jumqed ovre the lase
dogs.

The qick drown Fox Jumped
over the laisye bogs

the qvit BAK
FOX JUP ovne lase
DOG

The kquk braun foks
ovr the lase n bogs.

The cwik brown fox
jummt over
the lazeadog.

the wia broh foxs jut
ouver the Lase broh
bogs.

the aike fos
tuteb ocven the
lavy Dag.

The cwic brawn fox jumped
over the las dogs.

The KWIK
Broh Fox
Lympovn
The lashi bog

TheQkOOiKBROWh
FOX JumTOVer
TheLaceDog

the koio braoun Fox
iumnt ovr the
laze dog

Tel gick Braroo Fox jumt
ovr The losve Dog

READING

What dyslexia looks like in reading:

- slow and choppy

- skipping or switching small function words (*of, the, a, his, for, in, on*)

- skipping or switching of word endings (reading "scratch", "scratchy" or "scratches", when the word is *scratched* or "fun" when the word is *funny*)

- slow reading, even by people with great intelligence

- avoidance techniques employed when the need for reading aloud arises

- May add or leave off sounds, especially sounds of R, L, or N ("glaze" or "graze" for the printed word *gaze*, "split" for *splint*, "string" for *sting*, "fog" for *frog*)

- Ignores contractions (reading "did not" when the word is *didn't*) or changing parts of a contraction (saying "I'm" when the word is *I'll* or "won't" when the word is *wouldn't*)

Types of reading errors:

- starts and ends the same as the actual word

- shaped similarly to the actual word

- reversals/transpositions –
    - directionality confusion (bog / dog)
    - same letters, but in a different order (expect / except)

- poor reading, even on common words and words that have been seen over and over (who/how, where/were, want/what)

- lack of knowledge about the logic and structure of our language (reading "plake" for *place*, or "smoke" for *smock*)

- missing part of a blend (bl, nd) or digraph (th, sh, ch)

- little or no knowledge that letters are symbols that represent sound and the student has not used the letters at all, but has used memory, context clues, pictures, or a predictable storyline to make guesses

- confusing similar sounds, like /sh/ and /ch/ or /v/ and /f/

- a familiar piece of the word is recognized (the word is *every* but student says, "very", or the word is *this* and student says, "his")

- scrambling - same letters but in a completely different order

Students can hang in there and convince parents and teachers that they're "reading just fine!" by relying on pictures, context clues, memory for the visual overall shape of words, and their intelligence. But as text begins to be less predictable, words begin to increase in length, and pages include fewer and fewer pictures, reading becomes a huge challenge.

Taught as helpful "strategies", students actually use memory, context clues and pictures less as strategies and more as coping techniques. Any student who does not know how to decipher the written code on a page **has** to rely on those methods of guessing.

When students read silently to themselves, some errors make perfect sense, look right, and are grammatically correct, so they often go unnoticed by the student. Uncorrected errors can change the meaning of the story tremendously. When a student reads "did" when the word is didn't, or "mowing" when the word is moving or other mistakes like Mrs./Mr., shop/chop, expensive/extensive, squirrel/squall, farmer/framer, or explode/explore, it can mess with the meaning of a passage without the student even noticing. Even the switching of little words like *a* and *the* can make a huge difference in meaning. Then when students aren't able to answer questions about the passage or accurately summarize it, teachers are quick to blame a "comprehension problem" when actually a lack of decoding skill is the cause.

Having been read to and exposure to books does not always transfer to students becoming efficient readers.

♥ One girl has the letters *ink* in her last name. Despite knowing her last name, and seeing it and writing it frequently, she could not tell me the sound that the letters *ink* make when they are together (/eenk/, as in pink, think, sink), even when I circled back and showed her the letter combination to try again.

♥ Several parents have told me about working and working on a word on a page, reinforcing its appearance, letters, and pronunciation, only to turn the page to find the same word but in a different spot. To the child, it's like a new word and the work begins all over again.

There is overlap in the categories of the following examples. For example, a student read "disturb" when the word on the paper was *disrupt*. That could be an error of up/down confusion (b/p) **and** a scrambling of letters (turb/rupt). When a student reads "anger" for the word *enrage*, those words have similar meaning, so it could be categorized as a context clue error, or I could categorize it as a scrambling of the letters since other than an extra letter e, the two words have the same letters. When students read "from" for the word *form*, it would fit in the "being a similar shape" section or in the "transposing of letters/sounds".

Also, some of the "Student's attempt" and the "Actual word" can go either way. For example, I have observed students read "mouth" for the actual word *month*, so I might show *mouth / month* on the chart, but I have equally seen students read "month" for the printed word *mouth (month / mouth)*.

Starts and ends the same or similarly shaped

Since students have relied heavily on memory for visual shape and taking in a whole word all at once, their reading errors often look very similar to the printed word they are attempting to read. When I'm measuring phonics skills (matching the correct sound to the correct letter or letters) and present the letter combination *tch*, which actually represents **one** sound (/ch/) as in the words *ki<u>tch</u>en* and *ma<u>tch</u>*, most students will guess the word "teach" or "touch" which both start and end the same as *tch*.

The following errors happen often. Many of them have been repeated by multiple students:

Student's attempt / Actual word

look / took	likes / licks	flowers / follows
kitten / kitchen	girl / grill	house / horse
several, server, serve / severe	nest / next	trail / trial
quiet / quite	lost / lots	reach / react
traffic / tariff	rush / rust	found / fond
beach / bench	overcorrected / overreacted	look / lock
agreement / agent	winter / window	window / widow
fast / fact	when /then	scream / scram
watched/walked	truck / trunk	pray / pry
expert / export	peek / peck	hail / hall
crayon / canyon	child / chilled	project / protect
protect / predict	we're / were	called / could
there / these	looked / liked	how / now
want / won't	that / what	away / anyway
stared / started	countries / cities	floor / flowers
ball / bail	may / many	plenty / penalty
those / whose	began, beginning / being	minute / mint
chef / shelf	hurry / hungry	don't / dot
strangle / struggle	leader / ladder	first / fist
spray /spry	forest / frost	from / form
conscious / conscience / cautious		silly / sly

Transposition of letter position in a word - Other than reading "on" for *no* or "saw" for *was*, reading errors are rarely an exact reversal or mirror-image, but are a transposition in the way a letter is facing, a transposition of a few letters, or a transposition of sounds (as in student saying "stopped" for the printed word *spot*).

Student's attempt / Actual word

left / felt	from / form	sernom / sermon
sing / sign	single / signal	board / broad
stiff / sift	stopped / spot	Sydney / Cindy
consent / connect	license / silence	lost / lots
Texas / taxes	reverse / reserve	smile / slime
bottled / blotted	assume / amuse	fost / soft
snuck / sunk	feel / flee	stick / skit
unclear / nuclear	fastest / safest	using / suing
bowl / blow	spectacle / skeptical	amused / assumed

Transposition of a letter's direction (up/down or left/right)

Student's attempt / Actual word

mouth / month	Crappy / Crabby	tap / tab
photo / quote	Maple / Mabel	approve / above
big / dig	may / way	an...an...an...? / auditory
put / but	dog / bog	dad / bad
bear / dear	matchmaker / watchmaker	wigman / wigwam
dot / pot	cop,cod / cob	tribe / trip

Finding a familiar piece

People with dyslexia may leaving off or change word beginnings and endings (prefixes and suffixes), find a familiar piece, or make a guess based on just the first part of the word.

Student's attempt / Actual word

need / needed	should / shoulder	his / this
sleeping / asleep	fun / funny	did / didn't
Japanese / chimpanzee	hungry / hunger	wind / window
trip / stripe	does / doesn't	very / river
very / silver	xylophone / saxophone	create, creator / creature
lemon / lemonade	instructions / instrument	telephone / telegraph
company / community	library / liberty	fables / fabulous
across / acrobat	caught / caution	horse / horn
temporarily / temperature	clone / cyclone	quiet / quilt

Scrambling

When whole words are memorized for their appearance as objects (3D), then those words can be read upside-down, backwards, sideways, or even scrambled. This seems to be a cool skill, with some adult dyslexics telling me, "I can read perfectly fine when the words are upside down," but it can cause errors with multiple transpositions.

If you think I might have put word-pairs in this scrambling section by mistake, slow down and really examine them. For example, it might seem that filter/flirt do not belong here, but by carefully looking and comparing, you'll notice that the *sounds* of filter (/f/, /i/ /l/ /t/ /r/) are a scrambling of the *letters* of flirt, and although "miles/limestone" isn't an exact scramble, the first five letters are.

- When reading *-ild* (like *child, mild*), student said, "lid".

- When reading *-ung* (like *hung, sung*), student said "gun".

- The word *spot* can easily be confused with, "stop", "post", or "pots" (I've heard all three)!

Student's attempt / Actual word

skin / sink	sourced / scoured	leefelt / leaflet
pots / post	warned / warden	slump / splum (nonsense)
scared / sacred	fastest / safest	license / silence
reverse / reserve	smile / slime	never / nerve
eat / ate	trees / street	elevation / evaluation
miles / limestone	filter / flirt	act / cat
now / won	vote / veto	mittens / minutes
scratch / starch	sleep / spell	closest / closet
below / elbow	cloud / could	chin / cinch
wish / whisper	sugary / surgery	tish / this

When I learned in 2008 from a Susan Barton presentation called, "Dyslexia: Symptoms and Solutions" that reading errors aren't random, I started to pay closer attention to students' mistakes.

The following examples are fascinating and true stories of students being the ultimate unscramblers and they all had me saying, "WHOA!"

♥ If you had been there when a school student was reading a book with a character named *Abby* and you heard the student instead say, "Baby", you might be quick to dismiss it as a random, out-of-the-blue mistake. If you take a closer look at the two names, you'll make the same realization that I did: they have the exact same letters.

♥ The same is true when the same young girl said, "Andy" when the dog character's name was actually *Danny*.

♥ Several students have read "card" for the word *crab*. This shows letter transposition of the letters A and the R, but also shows left/right transposition of the letter b.

♥ A student read "blue" when the word was *duel*. If you consider left/right transposition of the b and d, then the word blue has the same letters as duel.

♥ Same with "anger" for the word *enrage*. My first guess was that this was a context/meaning error since the whole phrase was "did enrage the agent", but other than an extra e, the two words have the same letters, but scrambled.

♥ The printed word on the page was *out* and a student read "not". Let's compare side by side: not / out. Transpositions include up/down confusion (u/n) and scrambling of the letter order. Lest you think it was a young, reader making a mistake due to inexperience, it was a 16-year-old.

Most of my students have broken the habit of guessing, but since their brains *are* becoming more automatic, occasionally the old unscrambling skill kicks in instinctively, as you'll see in the following two stories that involve different teenagers in the later lessons of structured literacy instruction:

♥ While reading a story, a student looked at the word *layer* and said, "early".

♥ A middle-school student was given the nonsense word *nulabe* to read. Learning about silent-e syllables, he had been taught to first divide the word into its syllables: nu—labe. He would then know how to pronounce each piece depending on the syllable type and should successfully read, "**noo**-labe". Rather than divide it into syllables, he made an immediate attempt and said, "unable".

While they stumped me for a few seconds, I looked more closely and found in both examples that the printed word and the spoken word contained the exact same letters/sounds and recognized these students as ultimate unscramblers.

WHOA!

Guesses that "make sense in that spot":

Some of the following attempts may have similar parts or start/end the same, but most do not look visually similar at all.

Student's attempt / Actual word

mom / mother	horse / pony	kitty / cat
small / little	terrified / frightened	silence / stillness
hamster / guinea pig	getting / growing	smartest / wisest
ground / garden	lady / woman	sea / ocean
said / shouted	become friends / be friendly	create / construct
stars / sky	questioning / quizzing	hop / jump
guy / lad	story / legend	baby/little
favorite / special	couch / chair	greatest / largest
stairs / steps	stays / sits	home, hole / den
dump / drop	didn't / doesn't	a dinosaur / Tyrannosaurus Rex
contest / competition	snack / food	shouted / screamed
scared / afraid	caught / got	monster / nightmare
go / went	washing / cleaning	carrot / cabbage
station / center	mouse / rat	push / press
mail / letters	yelled / laughed	auntie / sister
under / around	gone / not here	cooking / making
hairy / furry	rabbit / mouse	money / cash

Errors such as these reveal that the student is neglecting information from the actual printed letters on the page, but instead is using context clues, picture clues, a predictable storyline and intelligence to guess a word that makes sense in that spot. Although context clues are needed in *some* situations (strong _wind_/_wind_ up the toy, _bow_ and arrow/took a _bow_) and they can *confirm* an attempt, using context clues to figure out an unknown word is very unreliable.

In the early grades, patterns and predictable story lines are meant to help scaffold until a student picks up language patterns and begins to decode by himself. Unfortunately, not only do the patterns often go unlearned, but reliance on these story patterns can make things worse, since students can *appear* to be reading.

♥ One first grade student relied on his memory of the story or its pattern. Often saying character names from other books, reading "Max and Ruby" for *Kate* and *James*, he also would get on a roll with the repeating pattern of, "I can see _____," found on most of the pages. So, when he reached a page starting with '*Look at...*,' he pointed and read, "I can see...". This student may or may not have had dyslexia, but his reading was similar to strategies employed by students who have not yet learned to get information from the printed text.

♥ Another predictable book told a story of young children at school, putting on different items of clothing in order to get ready for recess during the winter time. Most pages contained sentences such as "The children put on their mittens," or "The children put on their coats." When a student got to the page where "The children put on their hats," she made two guesses based on the pattern and the picture, before finally getting it right:

"The children put on their boots…shoes… hats."

She had not been taught even the most basic phonics, since neither guess relied on the actual letters of the word, which would have been way more helpful.

♥ Getting ready to begin structured literacy instruction with a 4th grade student, I asked him, "What do you do when you get to a tricky word?"

He answered, "I sound it out."

I imagined his parents and teachers telling him to "sound it out" when he got stuck. "Okay, tell me more," I prompted. "What do you mean by 'sound it out'?"

In all sincerity, the student answered, "Well, sounding it out means thinking really hard about what makes sense."

Some fellow educators and literacy trainers have expressed to me that since reading is about meaning, errors that don't change the "big idea" of the text are acceptable and not actually considered errors. For example, some educators would view it as perfectly normal and not a cause for concern when a child reads "rug" or "carpet" for the word *mat*, "said" for the word *shouted*, or "jump" for the word *hop*.

I agree that the ultimate goal of reading is understanding, but for that exact reason, I find it worrisome when a child cannot use the information that the printed text is giving. And since meaning IS the goal of reading, I would argue that although some errors may not change the main idea, they definitely can change the little details of a passage. Specifics and details give students a more accurate picture in their heads as they read and create true and full understanding of a passage.

♥ One student read "Sam made a <u>decision</u>." Although the guess makes perfect sense, sounds grammatically correct, and even looks similar to the printed word, the actual word on the page was ***declaration***.

Guessing by using context often turns into a bit of a Mad Lib story:

I saw a _____. (fill in any noun)

Mom is _____. (fill in any verb ending in *-ing*)

Consider the following sentence:

The family of foxes quickly ran back to the safety of their _____.

Although any of the following words would be considered "acceptable" by some, each convey a different picture in my head. Reading something different than the actual word could greatly affect the true meaning intended by the author.

home, den, hole, abode, house, habitat, shelter, hut, street, path, tree stump, cave, place, spot, nest, palace, shack, headquarters, space, neighborhood, territory, patch, lair, forest, area, tunnel, base, hillside, burrow, hideout, dugout, foxhole, nook, hollow, dwelling, bungalow, camp, niche, alcove, dungeon, chamber, field, hideaway, grove, thicket

♥ Before I knew about dyslexia and structured literacy, I was working with a bright 5th grader who was reading from a page of the Bill Peet book, *Big Bad Bruce*. He reached the word *shivered* and stopped. No amount of context, pictures, strategies (like skipping the word and then coming back), or even hints and coaching by me could bring the correct word to student's mind.

The book was filled with many magnificent words: **bedraggled, sprawled, haunches, snort, swirling, jittery, rippled, frowsy, tidbit, bruised, blunder, raucous, echoed, smithereens, dwindling, scurried, lumbered, brute, shriveling,** and **diminishing**, not to mention character names, sound effects, and nonsense words like **flumpity, bumpity, whump, kerplump, trizzle, blurps, whiffle, snuffling** and **ker-sploosh.**

Even for a student with good vocabulary, using context clues and pictures to "think of what would make sense" would not be very helpful for reading any of these words. And it's impractical (and frustrating for students) to have someone hovering over their shoulder while they read aloud, ready to jump in and help or tell them all the new or tricky words.

♥ One 1st grade student was trying to use meaning and other strategies she learned in Reading Recovery, but there was just no strategy I could teach her to help her with words in the story, like **awesome, magnifying, eyebrows, spies,** without just being told.

Rather than using meaning to figure out a word's pronunciation, it would be far more effective the other way around, first decoding to correctly pronounce the word and then using context and picture clues to figure out the meaning: "That word says 'shivered'. Based on the picture and what's going on in the story, what could 'shivered' mean?"

There are two fantastic options for students to access the rich vocabulary found in stories like Bill Peet's and J.K. Rowling's. One is to allow students to listen to the stories (audiobooks or someone reading *to* them). The other is to teach students *how* to read by using the structure and logic of words (letters, syllables, and word parts from left to right). Until students reach a level of proficient accuracy and fluency, a combination of both options is best: letting students listen to stories at their vocabulary and interest level, while at the same time, teaching them how to read by decoding.

WRITING and PENMANSHIP

What dyslexia looks like in written work:

- odd pencil grip
- written work often does not reflect intelligence and vocabulary levels
- poor spelling
- poor handwriting
- no use or awareness of the margins, with words starting toward the center or running all the way to the edge of the paper
- missing punctuation
- misuse of capital letters
- odd spacing between letters or words
- scribbled out or erased words, sometimes to the point of ripped paper
- short and safe passages, written with simple, easy-to-spell words or the *opposite*: pages and pages of creative, elaborate words, all misspelled and run-together with little or no punctuation or capitalization

Spelling overlaps into writing, as in this student's attempt at spelling the word **bank**. It shows a transposition, odd letter formation, letters that are not proportional, and a randomly added silent e:

bank

Writing is a daunting language task for students with dyslexia.

In regards to written expression, there are many moving parts to consider, each a challenge in and of itself: composing (thinking of what to say), organization, vocabulary (choosing which words to use), style (author's voice), grammar, spelling, and conventions (capitalization and punctuation), not to mention the actual act of writing or typing the words onto the paper.

The imagination, creativity, and intelligence needed to produce written work exists, but since writing involves so many language processing tasks, a student can quickly become overwhelmed at the thought of a writing assignment. Many students feel defeated before they even begin. They sit in front of a blank page of paper for long periods of time and sometimes aren't even able to get started.

Once they *have* written something, proof-reading/editing their own work proves to be almost impossible. Students often do not notice any errors or become discouraged over the red correction marks made by someone else.

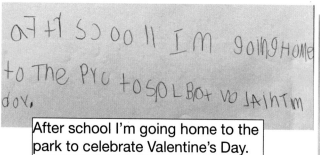

After school I'm going home to the park to celebrate Valentine's Day.

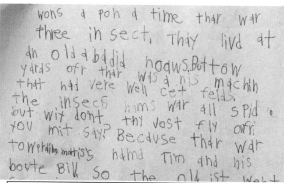

Once upon a time, there were three insects. They lived at an old abandoned house. But two yards over, there was a nice mansion that had very well-cut fields. The insects' names were all Spid. But why don't they just fly over, you might say? Because there were two praying mantises, named Tim and his buddy Bill.

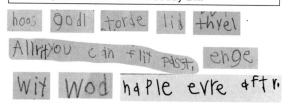

Later in the story: who's, gobble, third, lied, they'll, alright you can fly past, energy, why, would, happily ever after

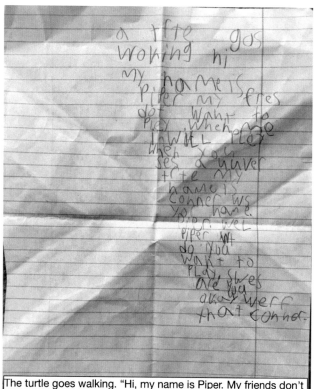

The turtle goes walking. "Hi, my name is Piper. My friends don't want to play with me."

"I will play with you," says another turtle. My name is Conner. What's your name?"

"Piper."

"Well, Piper, what do you want to play?"

"Swings. Are you okay with that Conner?"

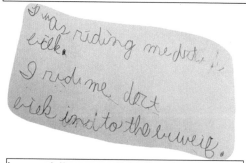

I was riding my dirt bike. I rode my dirt bike into the barbed wire fence.

Today I have a soccer game. I am so so excited about it. I hope we win.

Odd Pencil Grip

The following pictures showcase the unusual pencil grip of students. A pencil grip like one of these does not automatically mean that the person has dyslexia (I have seen a few people with a grip like this who did not have dyslexia), but it is interesting that almost *all* of my students have an odd grip, regardless of the neatness of their handwriting. Although the grips do vary, I learned from Susan Barton to notice one thing that they have in common: the thumb tends to extend over the top of the pencil. Rather than the thumb and index finger sharing control, the pencil movement is controlled by arm movements or the whole hand, causing the hand to cramp up or tire easily. Finding this both interesting and true, I began to snap pictures of students in the act of writing.

♥ As I brought my phone close to a middle school girl as she was writing, I told her, "Don't mind me, I'm just taking a picture of the way you hold your pencil when you write." She immediately relaxed her grip and switched to a 'normal' grip." After showing her the pencil grip photos I had taken of other students, many just like hers, she was surprised and relieved. "I thought I was the only one with a weird grip like that!"

Here are pictures of what dyslexia looks like in pencil grip:

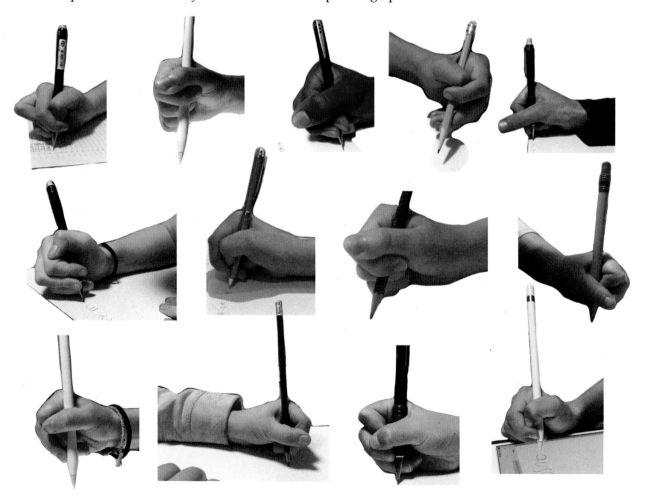

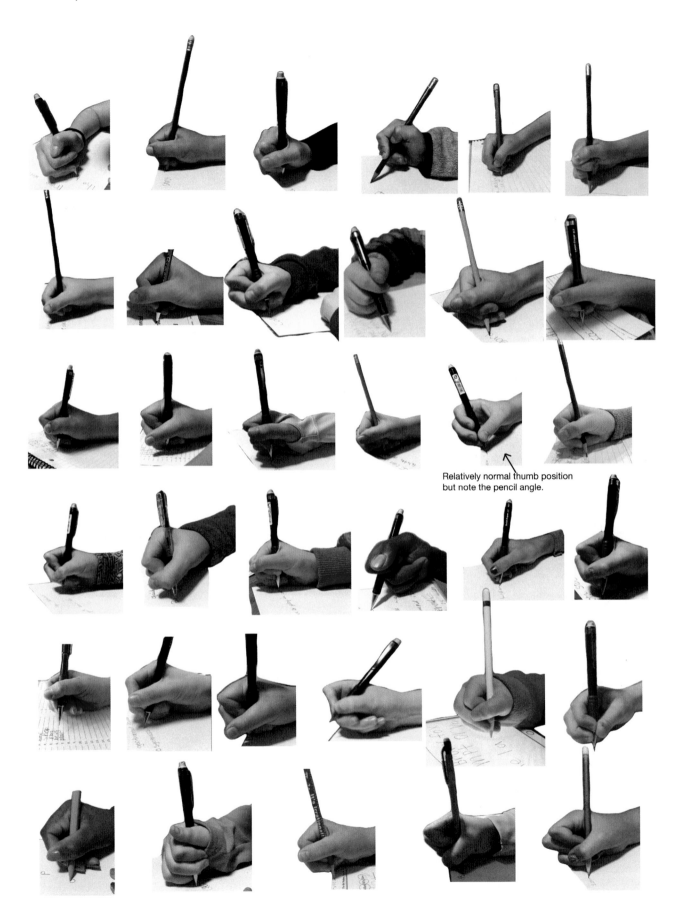

Relatively normal thumb position
but note the pencil angle.

Odd Letter Formation

What dyslexia looks like in letter formation:

- letters that don't sit on the line

- letters all the same size, with no ascenders (letter parts that go up tall, all the way to the top line) or descenders (letter parts that go down below the bottom line)

- letter reversals

- letters formed in odd, inefficient ways, like starting from the bottom and going up or using extra pencil strokes (a pencil stroke is each time a pencil makes a mark and then then is lifted to begin a new mark), and right-to-left strokes

- capital letters often used for the often-reversed letters like <u>b</u>, <u>d</u>, and <u>p</u>

- some letters drawn artistically, like an object, with arbitrary pencil strokes and varying starting points

Each letter of our alphabet can be formed efficiently by placing a pencil at a certain starting point, moving the pencil in a specific direction, and forming a few strokes in sequence. People with dyslexia who have not been explicitly taught how to form letters may form their letters starting in the "wrong" spot, going the wrong way, or making the right pencil strokes but in the wrong order. The resulting "drawing" may ultimately look like the intended letter, but its formation is inefficient and varied.

In general, students with dyslexia have a hard time remembering a sequence of steps, especially when they seem random. Letter formation is no different. While there is not necessarily a right or wrong way to form letters, there <u>is</u> a most-efficient, most-legible, least-likely-to-reverse way.

Efficient letter formation requires students to remember a specific sequence of steps for each letter, while also paying attention to directionality. Students must remember the starting point, the direction to go, when and where to lift the pencil, when to begin a new stroke, and how to finish one letter and move to the next.

Although I *do* give handwriting and letter formation tips, my main goal is to improve reading and spelling skills. Pencil grip and neatness are low on my priority list and largely ignored, especially with older students who come to me with poor handwriting. When letters have been formed incorrectly for so long, it becomes ingrained and very hard to fix.

Kevin   felt   frantic   candle

merciful   dribble   when   and   here

-7th grader

♥ This "simple" thank you note (pictured below) was likely not an easy feat.

- The letter **h** and the letter **n** in the word *thank* are the same shape and size
- The letter **k** appears to be two separate strokes of the pen and are not connected
- There are many extra strokes in the formation of the **y** in the word *you*
- There are capital letters mid-sentence, but neither the first word of the sentence nor his name is capitalized
- All the letters are about the same size, with no tall letters (**t, h, f**) or letters that descend below the line (**y, g**)
- Letters used more than once (**a, u, o, r,** and **y**) are made in varying ways
- Inconsistent spacing between letters and words

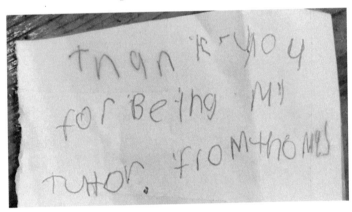

♥ The next examples were written by one of my most intelligent students. He had been diagnosed with Asperger's Syndrome, dyslexia, and dysgraphia. The odd letter formation, scratches, and scribbles could easily betray this student's intelligence, vocabulary, understanding of difficult topics, and amazing ability to learn. Soon after these pictures were taken, he began using the keyboard for his spelling and writing tasks.

Cursive

Because of odd letter formation and the use of right-to-left and bottom-to-top pen strokes, learning cursive can become a nightmare.

♥ One student told me that a substitute teacher had given an assignment and required it be written in cursive. The student was unable to do the assignment since he could not remember how to write in cursive.

Occasionally, the cursive writing I see is beautiful and flowing, but more often than not, it reminds me of someone trying to write a word on an Etch-a-Sketch.

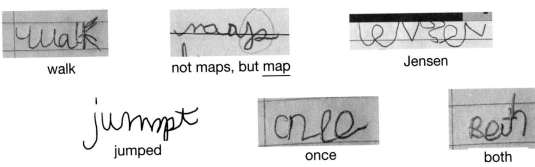

walk

not maps, but map

Jensen

jumped

once

both

Muscle memory or automatic mode

Muscle memory errors occur when students are so used to writing a certain letter or word that once they get started, their brain continues on autopilot and the letter or word that is written was not intended. An example of this would be if a person has been writing the number 8 several times and then tries to write the letter S, the person may continue on after the S is formed and accidentally form an 8.

Several students will say a sound or a letter and then write something completely different than they intended. Most of them realize it as soon as it's written, exclaiming to me, "Ack! I meant to write a _____. Did you see that?!"

Wrote a __W__. "I meant to write a __u__."

Wrote a __g__. "I meant to write an __a__."

Wrote a __n__. "I meant to write a __m__."

Letter stems

In the handwriting examples that follow, you'll notice that letters are often formed without their stem, or the stem is added as an afterthought. For example, the lowercase *r* can be made with one pencil stroke. Its most efficient formation begins at the top and moves straight down. Once the pencil reaches the bottom line on the paper, the pencil reverses course and heads back up the same line, curving to the right when nearing the top, naturally forming a stem. Some students completely disregard the stem; others draw the cane-looking part of the *r* and then go back and add a stem.

Most efficient

Or sometimes stems are added to letters (or numbers) that don't normally have stems.

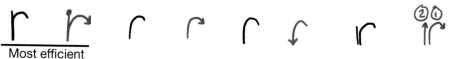

Backwards br? ...Backwards dr? ...Nope. It's an oddly formed 76.

Students sometimes DRAW certain letters in an artistic way and don't seem to be bothered by the extra time it takes.

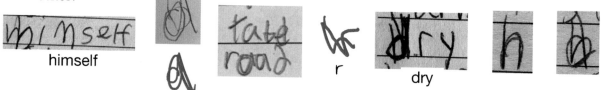

Rather than erase and correct, some students will just stack their writing attempts on top of each other.

himself

r

dry

Transpositions

Left/right and up/down transpositions can occur with just about every letter (and number).

♥ When first learning that the letter Y in middle of a silent e syllable represents the long-I sound, she wanted to write herself a reminder note above the letter Y in the word *Clyde*, but accidentally and without noticing, she wrote an exclamation mark (upside down, lowercase i).

Clyde

Here are a few less-common transpositions:

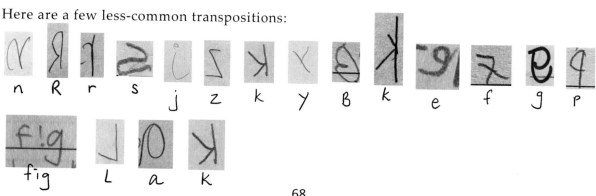

n   R   r   s   j   z   k   y   B   k   e   f   g   p

fig   L   a   k

When in doubt of a letter's direction, students sometimes use the following strategies:

- Use an uppercase/capital

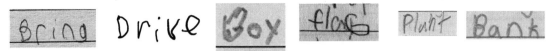

- Draw both letters, on top of each other

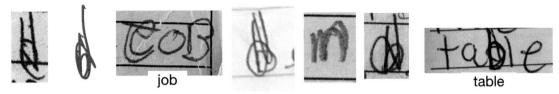

- Create a letter that could pass as either letter

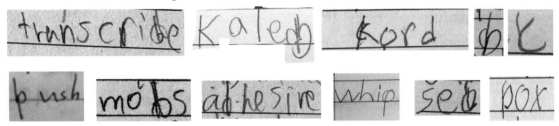

While most transpositions disappear after time or after structured literacy instruction, they occasionally still occur, even into adulthood.

Just like spelling and reading, penmanship and letter formation can be taught using explicit and systematic teaching and practice of certain motions. Most letters start at the top and many share the same beginning pencil stroke.

For information about one well-known method of teaching handwriting, see *Handwriting Without Tears* in Appendix C.

The next few pages are a compilation of the ABCs of letter formation. I include other letters of a word in some examples, just to show context or scale (or proof!).

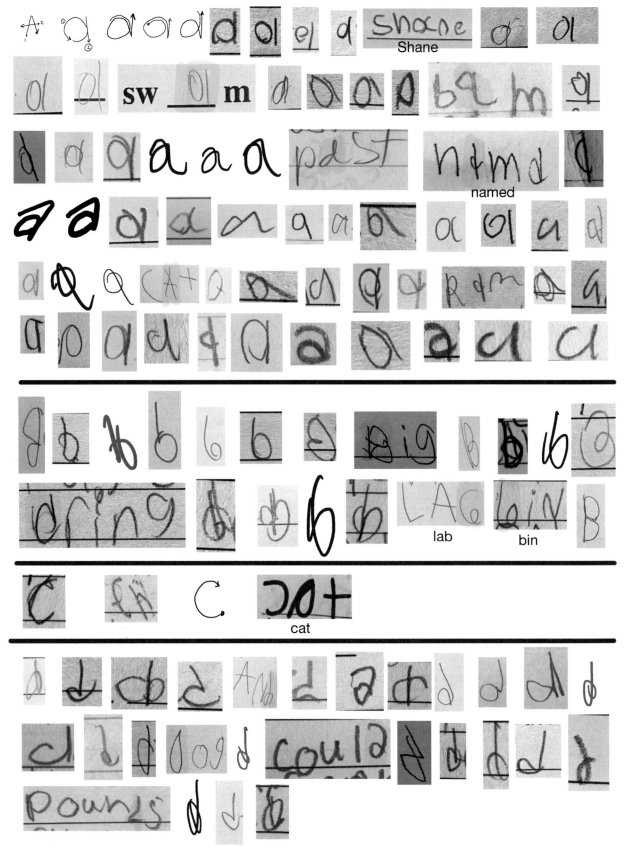

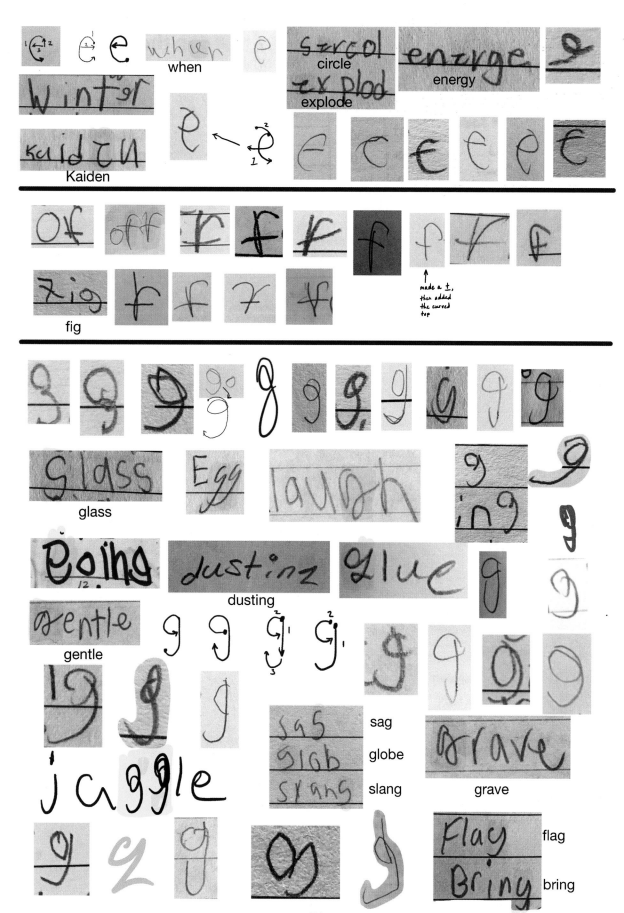

when

circle

explode

energy

Winter

Kaiden

fig

made a +,
then added
the curved
top

glass

Egg

laugh

ing

dusting

glue

gentle

sag

globe

slang

grave

flag

bring

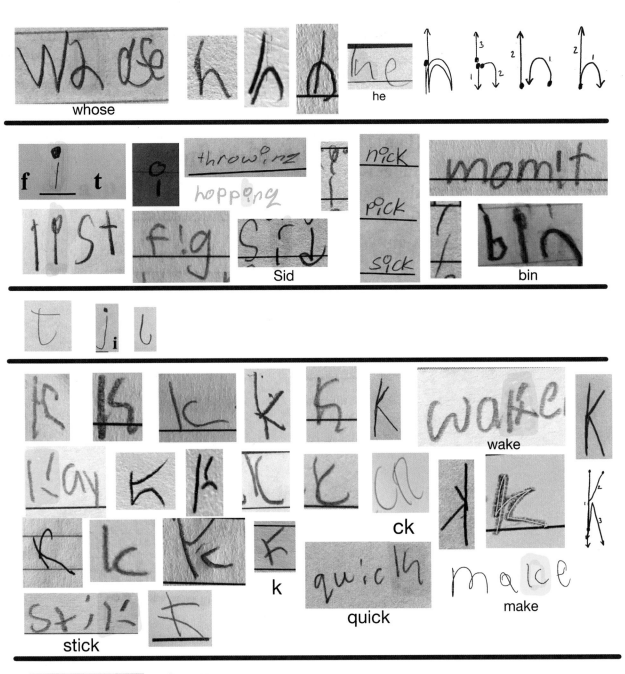

whose

he

throwing
hopping

f i t

nick
pick
sock

mom!t

Sid

bin

t j i

wake

ck

k

quick

make

stick

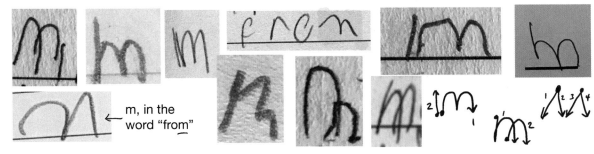

blink   lin (part of last name)

fren

m, in the word "from"

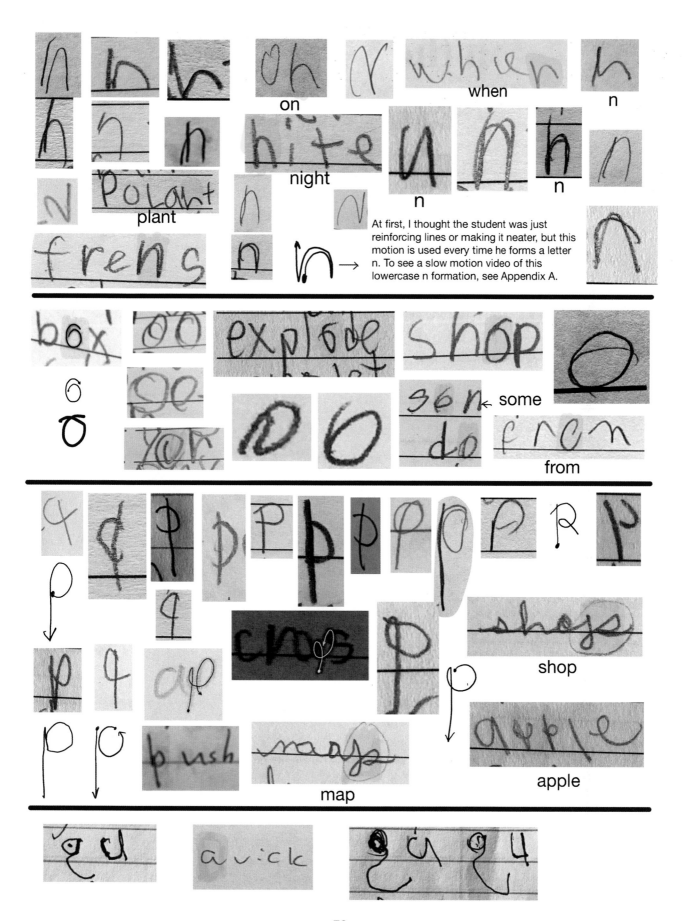

on

when

n

night

n

n

n

plant

At first, I thought the student was just reinforcing lines or making it neater, but this motion is used every time he forms a letter n. To see a slow motion video of this lowercase n formation, see Appendix A.

frens

some

from

shop

apple

push

map

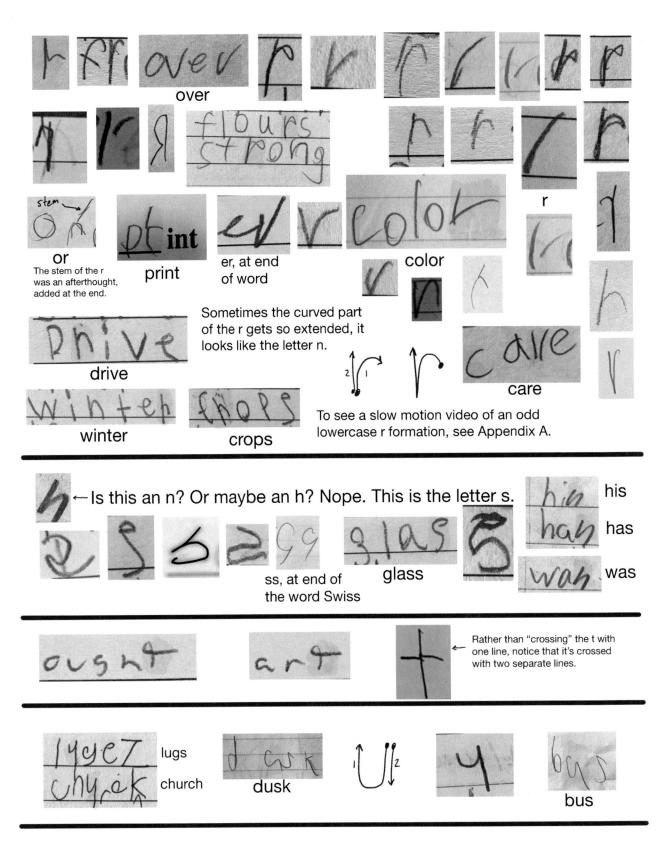

over

stem →

or

The stem of the r
was an afterthought,
added at the end.

print

er, at end
of word

color

r

Sometimes the curved part
of the r gets so extended, it
looks like the letter n.

drive

care

winter   crops

To see a slow motion video of an odd
lowercase r formation, see Appendix A.

←Is this an n? Or maybe an h? Nope. This is the letter s.

his

has

ss, at end of
the word Swiss

glass

was

Rather than "crossing" the t with
one line, notice that it's crossed
with two separate lines.

ought   art

lugs

church

dusk

bus

The nice thing about the letter V is that you can form it from right-to-left
or left-to-right and no one will be the wiser.

74

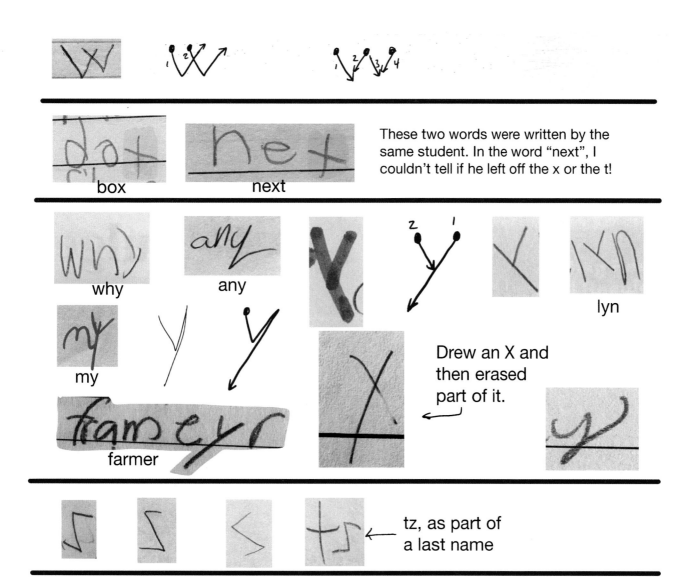

box

next

These two words were written by the same student. In the word "next", I couldn't tell if he left off the x or the t!

why

any

lyn

my

farmer

Drew an X and then erased part of it.

tz, as part of a last name

SPEECH

What dyslexia looks like (actually what it sounds like) in speech:

- late to talk

- may have a hard time saying longer words

- often mixes up the sounds and syllables of words, when speaking

- subtle mispronunciations of words or sayings (instead of "chomping at the bit", saying "biting at the bit")

- may have a hard time finding the right word to say, despite having a good vocabulary and a complete understanding of the meaning of the word.

- may confuse one word with another word that has a similar part

- confuses similar-sounding sounds or trouble making certain sounds

- leaves off a sound, like saying "fustrated" rather than "frustrated"

- may transpose the sounds, syllables, or even whole words

Since the "lexia" part of dyslexia means "language", difficulty can show up in all areas of language including the act of saying words. Sometimes students are aware of their mispronunciations or misuse of words and sometimes not.

♥"I'm on a more extreme side of the symptoms with language recall. My family calls it my own language, because I have words that I've made up that I am very certain about what the word means. I'll use really complex words, inappropriately, in sentences and I think it makes total sense." –M.H., Educator

Longer Words

Three different students had trouble pronouncing the word "shoulder". One of them knew he was mispronouncing it. He kept pointing to his shoulder to prove that he knew it, but his mouth kept saying, "soldier".

bisketti / pasketti (spaghetti)   ambliance (ambulance)

dillexia (dyslexia)   breftist (breakfast)

mazagine (magazine)   necksaliss (necklace) barella or unbrella   (umbrella)   basept   (except)

calapitter   (caterpillar)   pacific vs. specific (both hard to say)

excape   (escape)   hossible (hospital)

ivy-profen (ibuprofen)   fercifikit (certificate)

/f/ and /th/ confusion
death (deaf)
althabet (alphabet)
golden retriether (golden retriever)
fum (thumb)
thireworks (fireworks)
inthinity (infinity)

Since /th/ and /f/ are commonly confused sounds, words that contain *both* /th/ and /f/ can be incredibly hard to pronounce, like *theft* and *thrift*.

/f/ and /v/ confusion
devective (defective)
evectively (effectively)
felocity (velocity)

m and n visual or sound confusion
ginnastics (gymnastics)
naybe (maybe)
unbrella (umbrella)
renember (remember)
vanpire (vampire)

Even when the /m/ and /n/ sounds are **spoken**, not even within a word, they are easily swapped by the brain. When practicing the skill of sequencing, I ask students to repeat back the three sounds, "Mmm...Nnn...Mmm". On multiple occasions, students repeated the sounds back as "Nnn...Mmm...Nnn".

Since /m/ and /n/ are commonly confused sounds, words that contain *both* /m/ and /n/ can be incredibly hard to pronounce. The most difficult and most common tongue twisters for people with dyslexia seem to be the ones that contain the letter m *and* the letter n, like *minimum, synonymous,* and the ones below. The /m/ and the /n/ are notoriously switched.

fenimine (feminine)	crinimal (criminal)
emeny (enemy)	aminal (animal)
pernament (permanent)	donimo (domino)
tourmanent (tournament)	cimmanon (cinnamon)
donimant (dominant)	miminum / minimun (minimum)
ecomonize (economize)	symonyn / synomyn (synonym)
tsumani (tsunami)	both anonymous and unanimous are tricky

Similar sounding, but not quite right

Students sometimes have an "ah ha" moment and realize their mispronunciations once they are able to read the word in print or have to say it slowly or start with the base-word to correctly spell it (like starting with *suppose* and then adding suffix *-ed* and suffix *-ly* for suppos**ed**ly).

Dark Vader (Darth Vader)	I'm dunna (I'm gonna/I'm going to)
seedweed… (seaweed)	Octover (October)
unrace, rerace, re-ace (erase)	summereen (submarine)
All timers…(Alzheimer's)	morneen, seeneen (morning, singing)
jampionship (championship)	insteresting (interesting)
intil (until)	bolf (both)
enscape, excape (escape)	acleast (at least)
cuv-erd (cupboard)	nusing (using)
type rope (tightrope)	pyramid (period)
chickmunk (chipmunk)	fly swapper (fly swatter)

counsint (cousin)

extruction workers (construction workers)

prensel (pretzel)

betend (pretend)

Intendo DS (Nintendo DS)

proglem (problem)

mustachios (pistachios)

apposed to be (supposed to be)

Verbal Muscle Memory?

This probably happens to everyone at some point, but even more so for people with dyslexia: their brains get geared up and start taking a run at saying a word or phrase and then what ends up coming out is not what was intended. To give a little example, since the two phrases start the same, I had a hard time saying "senior picnic" since my mouth kept wanting to say "senior picture".

♥ A student said, "post officer", meaning just *post office*.

♥ A student was trying to explain that he got a *paper cut*, but said, "paper clip".

Similar sounding parts can also cause confusion between phrases or names. I confused the names of two moms who I met around the same time, one with the first name *Darlene* and one with the last name *Darling*.

♥ One middle schooler thought *phonemic awareness* was a disease because of common events and fundraisers for "cancer awareness".

♥ "It's a big joke in my family. My dad cannot call me by my name the first time. I can't call my son either. I go through my all five brothers and my other son before I talk to my son, Brandon. "Zach, Brian, Brandon...," it gets so frustrating, but my dad does the same thing. He'll call whoever he's talking to five different names before he gets to the right name. It's very frustrating for them but it can come up very funny for us." –G.M., Civil Engineer

Similar parts or sound very similar:

said "porcu**pine**" ——————————— meant **pine** cone

said "Cost**co**" ——————————— meant Shop**Ko**

said "Shoe **Goo**" ——————————— meant **Goo** Gone

said "Mill**stone**" ——————————— meant **Stone**wall Jackson's

said "toothpicks" ——————————— meant Q-tips

said "manager" ——————————— meant janitor

said "**veterin**arian" —————————————— meant **veteran**

said "they yelled into the big homo**phones**"—— meant mega**phones**

said "com**ponent**" —————————————— meant op**ponent**

said "we packed hot cocoa in a **thermos**tat"—— meant **thermos**

said "therm**ometer**" —————————————— meant speed**ometer**

an adult said "com**ponent**" ——————————she thought it meant "op**ponent**"

said "Popeye wore a wheel **barr**ow" ————— meant "**barr**el"

said "flash**light**" —————————————— meant night**light**

Transposed sounds, syllables or words:

Sometimes students are aware of their tongue twist ("Headfore...I mean fedhore. ACK! I mean forehead!!") and other times they do not even notice, like a girl telling me about her trip to "Wa-hi-ee" (meant Hawaii).

said "**h**air **b**ug" ——————— meant **b**ear **h**ug

said "edder oudges" ——————— meant outer edges

said "ficture perst" ——————— meant picture first

said "Yew Nork" ——————— meant New York

said "tie shoeing" ——————— meant shoe tying

said "f**ur**n**ace**" ——————— meant th**erm**o**s**

said "marote" ——————— meant remote

said "brefkest" ——————— meant breakfast

said "wirefuud" ——————— meant firewood

said "wops" ——————— meant wasp

said "oval" ——————— meant olive

said "To-haw" ——————— meant Tahoe

said "Hermit the Crab" ——————— meant Kermit the Frog

said "headfore" ——————— meant forehead

said "bist-rands" ——————— meant wristbands

said "wall in the hole"———————meant "hole in the wall"

said "curfiss" ———————meant cursive

said "saulf -alarm"———————meant false alarm

said "stain tration" ——————— meant train station

said "Saragota"——————— meant Saratoga

said "oppucation"——————— meant occupation

said "Clover's"——————— meant Culver's

said "coo-tan"——————— meant toucan

said "ramoon"——————— meant maroon

People with dyslexia may have a hard time finding the right word to say, despite having a good vocabulary and a complete understanding of the word for which they are searching. They can picture the word, but just cannot retrieve its name, so they may point, gesture, use words like "thingy", try to describe it, or even invent a new name for it.

- "thing that water comes out of…" (faucet)
- "part between the sidewalk and the street that fills with water when it rains…" (gutter)
- "type of show that has sketches…" (cartoons)
- "piece of sidewalk you jump your bike off of…(curb)
- "squeezy snake" (boa constrictor)
- "new roof…sun window" (sun roof)
- "exciting mark" (exclamation mark)
- "stopping sign" (stop sign)
- "the over-the-river crossy thing" (bridge)
- While adding the dot on a lowercase letter i, a student said, "period".
- "stew thing" (crock pot)
- One girl was trying to name a type of candy. "It starts with an S… not Snickers… not Skittles." "No, not Smarties (on my suggestion) … not chocolate…Yes, STARBURSTS!"
- "stuff you can tear off" (velcro)
- "toilet got plogged" (cross between plugged and clogged?)

♥ "All dyslexics that I know play the game *"Guess That"* with their family and with everybody they know. So if I'm talking to my daughter and I want her to go get something for me, I can't think of what it is called, but I have a visual picture of it so I'll be like, "Can you get the thing that's in the cupboard that takes your polish off your nails?"…(nail polish remover) --M.H, Educator

OTHER SIGNS and CURIOSITIES

This section is full of "other" signs of dyslexia. Just like with every other section of this book, not everyone with dyslexia will experience all the items listed in this section.

Trouble memorizing - Unless students see the logic behind it, they may have trouble memorizing a list or a sequence of steps, such as months of year, days of week, order of the alphabet (without using the song), steps of long division, steps of tying shoes, and basic math facts.

Anxiety and depression

Poor self-esteem, doubt their abilities

Trouble with math – Although some students excel in math and have an understanding of math concepts, there are many aspects of math that often give people with dyslexia grief:

- showing their work/thinking after figuring out the solution to a problem visually or by its pattern

- memorizing basic math facts

- sequencing (remembering all the many steps of a problem and following them in the right order)

- directionality (reading "72" for 27 or knowing which way to carry a number)

- thinking linearly

- reading the directions or the story problems to see what actually needs solving

- greater than and less than symbols (>, <)

- concepts of time

Perfectionism – Sometimes when a person with dyslexia thinks that there is a good chance that they can't do a task well, then they do not want to even start or attempt the task. This can be misunderstood as laziness or lack of motivation.

Low confidence

Late to establish a dominant hand – People with dyslexia are often ambidextrous, use different hands for different tasks, or use both hands simultaneously. One student told me she was right-handed and then proceeded to leave her right hand in her lap for pulling, tapping, and manipulating tiles.

Difficulty learning a foreign language – American Sign Language (ASL) is a good alternative that is often accepted for high school foreign language credit requirements. I learned from one high school student that he was enjoying sign language classes since there are no reversals in sign language (the hand motions and signs can be made with either hand) and there are no small function words like *is*, *of*, *a*, and *the*.

I know that names often do not always follow spelling rules, but do parents accidentally give clues to their *own* dyslexia when they spell their children's names without following some "normal" spelling rules?

- Dav (Dave) Pilkey – author of the Captain Underpants series
- Jil (Jill) – my college roommate (who was intelligent, knew sign language, and had atrocious spelling)
- Halley – Based on syllable types, this name should be pronounced either HAH-lee (short a sound, like apple) or HALL ee (all like mall/fall). Instead, though, it is "HAY lee".
- Joeseph (Joseph)
- Kelle (Kelly)

Trouble telling time on a clock with hands – A friend of mine is dyslexic and a recently published author. She told me that a visitor to her home once commented, "None of the clocks on your wall are set to the right time!"

"Oh, I can't read those types of clocks! They are all just for decoration!"

Difficulty taking notes during a lecture

Can be stubborn (in a good way) **and show grit and perseverance** – When told that there is something that is impossible for them or there is a goal that they can't meet, (go to college, get a certain job, pass a class, learn a skill) look out! They will work hard and find a way to prove the statement or the person wrong.

Only half right - One boy says "butter" when referring to peanut butter, and an adult I know has confused many people (at first) since he refers to hot chocolate as just "chocolate".

Family members with dyslexia

May also have ADD or ADHD – Many students with dyslexia also have <u>A</u>ttention <u>D</u>eficit <u>D</u>isorder with or without <u>H</u>yperactivity, which can affect memory, focus, and organization skills, among other things.

Slow at "rapid naming" – Just like other signs, not all students exhibit difficulty in rapid naming. For a "Rapid Naming" test, students are just asked to name simple items on a page as rapidly as they can. The items are simple and well-known, since this is not a test of knowledge, but one of brain processing, essentially testing how fast students can bring each item's name to mind and then speak it. Items might include, numbers, letters, colors, or pictures of simple objects, like a ball, table, chair, key, and a star. There might be 25-30 items on a page, but it's usually just 5 or 6 items, randomly repeated to fill a full page.

Once it is verified that the student can identify each item correctly, then they are presented a whole page of the items and asked to name them as quickly as they can.

A good rapid naming test for parents might be to show individual pictures of each of their children and ask them to name them ("Of course I know all my children's names! That's Jenny, Brandon, Joseph and Megan."). Then, present a page filled with different sequences of the pictures and ask the parents to start at the top and go from left to right, naming each child as quickly as possible. Some parents might be completely fluent at this "naming" task, but others will be slow, choppy, and have a few mistakes sprinkled in: "Je...Br...Joseph! Brandon.   Megan.   Jo... Menny, I mean Jenny!"

There is not too much that can be done to speed up brain processing speed, but it clearly has nothing to do with intelligence or knowledge. Rapid naming scores can give good information for educators and can identify students who could use **more time**.

- Extra time to work through an assignment or take a test.
- Time to think through the wording of something they'd like to say.
- More time to practice and learn new skills.
- Time to process what's being asked and formulate an answer in their heads before saying it out loud.

Have a hard time copying from another paper or from the board – In addition to being slow at tasks of copying, the student will lose his place frequently and will misspell words that are spelled correctly "right in front of him".

Confuse directions left and right

Critical thinking and deeper insight into stories (that are read TO them)

Difficulty reading sheet music – Although some people with dyslexia exhibit strengths in the area of music, they often memorize or play the songs by ear.

Long nights of homework filled with tears and battles

Twins – one with dyslexia, one without

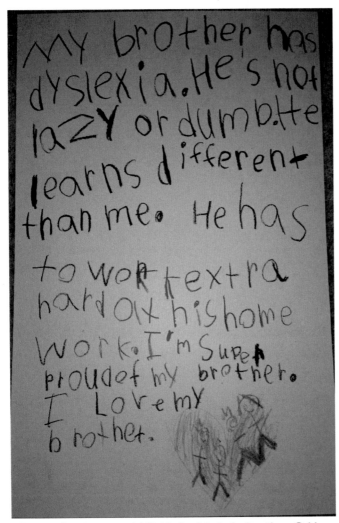

My brother has dyslexia.
He's not lazy or dumb.
He learns different
than me. He has to work
extra hard at his
homework. I am super
proud of my brother. I
love my brother.

Poster by 6-year-old B.H. for his twin brother G.H.

Trouble learning to tie shoes – Tying shoe laces involves sequencing and directionality. Do I loop this lace first or this one? Does this go over or under?

Frequent ear infections

Trouble recognizing or producing words that rhyme – Other than parroting common rhyming words that they have heard over and over in nursery rhymes and have memorized, many students are unable to rhyme. Rhyming is often taught under the guise of "word families" (like the *-at* family: cat/hat/mat/fat) or as words that have the same letters at the end, but rhyming is really about *sounds*. Some words that are spelled with the same letters at the end *don't* rhyme, like *primate* and *climate*, and some words that are spelled differently at the end *do* rhyme like *sew, toe, no,* and *grow*. In order to rhyme, students must have enough phonemic awareness to be able to add to, drop, or swap out the consonant sound/sounds at the beginning of a word.

♥ "What rhymes with plane?"
"Helicopter"

♥ A 5th grader read me his poetry:
"Roses are Red
Violets are Blue
Do you like my poem?"

Do things differently - Whether it be computer shortcuts, completing chores more efficiently, or just being unique, if there is a different-but-better way of accomplishing a task, my students will find it.

Doodles, fiddles, and daydreams – These actions can appear as though the student is off-task or not listening. While that may sometimes truly be the case, doodling and fiddling can help a student focus. When daydreaming, a student may be inventing, analyzing, problem-solving, or dreaming about the next great idea or project.

STRATEGIES USED TO HIDE DYSLEXIA

When I was in 5th grade, I was excited that I had been invited over to a new friend's house. I was anxious to make a good impression since I was in awe of this girl because she was in the *6th grade*. She was pretty and popular and she knew all the "cool older kids". While hanging out at her house, she gestured to the radio in her room (no iTunes, Pandora, or Spotify at that time) and suggested I turn it to a good station. This sent me into panic-mode. I knew the *names* of the popular radio stations and I knew all the good songs of the day, but I didn't know the *numbers* of the stations. In fact, I did not often listen to a radio at my house so I didn't really even know how to turn the dial to tune in to specific stations. Rather than let on to the fact that I had no clue what I was doing, I acted like the radio was full of static and pretended that no stations were coming in clearly as I wildly turned the radio dial back and forth.

Just like I was trying to save face, so do people with dyslexia. Since they are deathly afraid of anyone finding out that they struggle to read, write, and spell, they are extra creative when it comes to hiding their struggles from everyone around them.

♥ "Can I tell you something?" a young girl confided. "I don't really like an audience [when reading aloud]. I get stage fright."

♥ "On days when I am tired, it is still hard to cover," said a successful computer and electrical engineer of hiding his dyslexia. He noted that his fears remain and flood back when he is asked to read aloud to his kids. "All those fears are coming back as I am required to do what I dread the most -- read out loud books like "Green Eggs and Ham" on a nightly basis."

♥ A local physician commented that even though he made it through all the classes and tests of medical school and has a successful career, the struggles and hiding continue into adulthood. He hopes that as communities gain awareness into dyslexia and the instruction that best helps eliminate the reading and spelling difficulties that go along with it, others won't feel the need to hide their dyslexia.

♥ I've learned of an adult who carried a sling around with him in his car. If he was going anyplace where he would be required to fill out a form or application, he would don the sling so he could use it as an excuse for someone else to fill out the form for him.

♥ A college graduate and inventor said this: "I pretended to read in elementary school. I'd sit with the book open in front of me and pass my finger under the words so that people (my parents, teachers, friends, siblings) wouldn't think I was dumb or lazy." - Cliff Weitzman, inventor of a text-to-speech app called Speechify. For more information, see *Cliff Weitzman*, Appendix C.

Never underestimate the creativity of someone trying to hide a weakness from their peers and teachers. To see an extreme example, look up books or videos by John Corcoran, who went through school, got a degree, and taught for 17 years without being able to read or write, or see *John Corcoran*, Appendix C.

Here are some strategies that I've seen employed by children, teenagers, and adults, to hide their reading and writing difficulties:

Strategies to hide reading difficulty

Pretend to be reading silently

- stare at an open book

- point and move finger from left to right

- regularly turn a page

Carry around big thick books

Blame eyesight

- "I forgot my glasses."

- act like it's blurry

- will rub eyes

- blink a lot

- adjust hat

- adjust glasses

- shake head

- pretend something is in their eye

Count ahead to see what section they will have to read aloud, and then try to prepare

Act naughty

Pretend to be sick

Memorize a reading passage or book

Cause a distraction

- ask a question

- make a "connection" to the reading passage and start telling the connection/story

- have a meltdown

- say or do something that makes people laugh

Pretend to need to use the restroom

Act stubborn or rebellious

- "This is too easy."

- "This is dumb."

- "I just don't want to."

Act as if they were right all along, even if they never say the unknown word

- "I knew it! I should have just said it."

Blame the hearing of others

- "That's what I said. You just didn't hear me."

Pretend to have lost their place

Blame their voice

- clear throat

- mumble or talk very quickly through the unknown words

- blame something in their mouth (braces, a lost tooth, retainers, candy, gum, food) for not being able to pronounce a word or for not talking clearly

- act like the word is a tongue twister and hard to pronounce: "Wi...wiss...wass.../w/... I know the word; I just can't say it" (was)

Try to go unnoticed

- stay extra quiet

- sit directly behind someone else to stay out of sight so as not to be called on

- hide

- go to the bathroom and stay there for long periods of time

VALUE OF SEEING

Recognizing and naming dyslexia has many merits:

- Learning that there is concrete evidence and a reason for their struggles usually comes as a relief to people who have experienced dyslexia.

- Students can rest in knowing that they have a normal (smart) brain.

- No time has to be wasted, since the best kind of language instruction for students with dyslexia is clear (and detailed in the next section).

- It gives permission to take focus off of the weaknesses and on to strengths and abilities (intelligence, creativity, innovation, logic…).

- People can make sense of some difficulties (Text from young adult: "Mom, the other day I saw *CMG* and processed it as GMC before I processed it as CMG. LOL!").

- Students can set their jaw with a sense of determination and resolve, at the hurdles that lie ahead, knowing that with hard work and perseverance, success is possible.

- Knowing that it's dyslexia gives struggles a purpose and helps students prepare for the stresses of life, through which strong character is built.

- There is value in knowing that there are many other people with dyslexia who share similar strengths and struggles.

- Individuals feel more comfortable sharing about their experiences with others, and can go easy on themselves and have a sense of humor about what makes them unique.

- People can learn to appreciate and even enjoy their differences.

WHAT TO DO

As mentioned in the "Reversals/Transpositions" section of this book, each part of language (reading, writing, spelling, and speech) is highly dependent on *sound*. Therefore, the type of instruction that builds the strongest readers and spellers begins with a focus on *sounds* and *how* to process them.

Through a systematic set of lessons that first builds phonemic awareness followed by explicit and cumulative teaching on the structure and logic of our language, a person's brain can be trained on how to efficiently process sounds for good reading and spelling.

Students are taught to spell by carefully listening to the sounds and word parts within spoken words and then using rules to correctly record a symbol (letter or letters) for each sequential sound. They are taught to read by being taught about and giving attention to the structure of words (letters, syllables, and word parts in order from left to right) rather than relying on context clues, picture clues or memorization.

Effective curriculum or methods include words like, *Orton-Gillingham, The Science of Reading, Synthetic Phonics, Evidence-Based,* or *Structured Literacy* and include instruction on phonemic awareness, phonics, syllable types, accenting patterns, morphology, and etymology in a way that is systematic and explicit. To see a graphic that shows how Structured Literacy helps *all* students (dyslexia or not), see **Nancy Young** in Appendix C.

The most effective instruction is also reciprocal. Reading and spelling are highly related, so it makes sense to teach them together. As the reading skills go up, so do the spelling skills. As the spelling skills increase, so do the reading skills.

Structured Literacy Terms

Systematic - According to the dictionary on lexico.com, the word *systematic* means "done or acting according to a fixed plan or system; methodical". Synonyms include *structured, methodical, organized, planned, well-ordered, logical,* and *efficient*. Systematic teaching is not just giving students "strategies" and "tricks", nor teaching skills randomly, as they come up while a child is reading. Systematic instruction means giving a series of lessons that follow a planned-out and sequential path, starting with the most basic or common and gradually working to more advanced skill levels.

<u>Explicit</u> – Rather than hoping they pick up on the patterns and rules of our language by exposure to words in a book or on a spelling list, students are clearly TOLD the reasons why words are pronounced or spelled the way they are.

<u>Cumulative</u>

The teaching starts with a solid foundation of sound (phonemic awareness) and the most basic and common of reading and spelling skills before gradually increasing in difficulty. Growing efficient and accurate readers and spellers is much like building a tower with blocks. New skills are built upon previously learned skills. Review and practice widen and strengthen the foundation and allow for a solid structure that is growing taller and stronger each day.

<u>Phonemic Awareness</u> – Phonemes are the smallest unit of sound within spoken words. Being aware of those phonemes and knowing that they can be removed, added, or changed to make new words is called *phonemic awareness*. For a refresher on phonemic awareness, refer back to page 32-35 of the "Reversals/Transpositions" section.

<u>Phonics</u> - I like to think of phonics as just the rules and logic of how spoken sounds and word parts are recorded on paper. The sound /ee/ might be heard at the end of a word, but students are told that rather than using the letter E, the /ee/ sound at the end of a word is spelled with the letter Y (cand<u>y</u>, luck<u>y</u>). Ears might hear /k/, but phonics knowledge is what helps to know whether to record that sound as the letter C in the words <u>*c*at</u> and *pi<u>c</u>nic*, CK in the words *sli<u>ck</u>* and *bra<u>ck</u>et*, or K as in <u>*kitten*</u>, *sil<u>k</u>*, and *bas<u>k</u>et*. Ears might hear /shun/ at the end of a word, but it's phonics that makes it known to spell /shun/ as TION in the word *vaca<u>tion</u>*, SION in the word *pen<u>sion</u>*, or SSION in the word *mi<u>ssion</u>*.

Knowing phonics also helps with reading. For example, students are told that the letter C usually represents /k/ (**c**at, **c**ut, **c**ot, secret, picnic), but if it is followed by an E, I, or Y, the letter C makes its less common sound, /s/ (**c**ity, ni**c**e, re**c**eive, **c**yclone). Also, students are taught how to pronounce the similarly spelled words *devi<u>c</u>e* and *devi<u>s</u>e*.

<u>Syllable Types</u> - Knowing how to divide a word into its syllables and then understanding each type of syllable gives valuable information about the sound that a vowel will make. Syllable knowledge helps students read, spell, and know the difference between words like Eddie/Edie, dinner/diner, griping/gripping, scar/scare, toll/tall, and snack/snake.

<u>Accenting Patterns</u> - Every word has an accented syllable. Sometimes called the "stressed" syllable, an accented syllable is the part of the word that is given more emphasis when spoken. I tell students that an accented syllable has more power and oomph to it, like the

first syllable in **PEN-cil** and the last syllable in **Bra-ZIL**. Knowing which syllables are accented and which are not can help read and spell words.

<u>Morphology</u> - Morphology is the study of form and structure. In language, morphology is the study of the form and structure of words and word parts. A morpheme is a word part that carries meaning. The word **dogs** has two morphemes: **dog** (animal) and **-s** (more than one). Words, Latin roots, Greek combining forms, prefixes, and suffixes are all word parts that hold meaning.

For example, the word ending **-ed** carries the meaning "in the past" and can make three sounds depending on the last sound of the word to which it's added: /t/ as in jumped, /d/ as in sailed, and /ed/ as in landed or lasted. Reading and spelling with suffix **-ed** requires knowledge of some rules (carry → carried, rat →ratted, rate→rated).

The word, astronaut, is made up of two morphemes:

astro = outer space

naut = sailor or traveler

It's fun to think of an astronaut as a "space sailor", one who navigates and travels in space.

Understanding morphemes and how they work helps reading, spelling, and comprehension.

<u>Etymology</u> - Etymology is the study of a word's origin. This helps explain the pronunciation, spelling, and meaning of words in our language that originate from other countries or are very old English words. Knowledge of etymology explains things like the fact that CH says /ch/ in English words (<u>ch</u>air, <u>ch</u>op, lun<u>ch</u>), /k/ in words that came from the Greek language (<u>ch</u>emistry, stoma<u>ch</u>, a<u>ch</u>e), and /sh/ in words that came from the French language (<u>ch</u>ef, ma<u>ch</u>ine, qui<u>ch</u>e).

Explicit and systematic teaching of the structure and logic of our language makes for strong readers and spellers and is actually quite fascinating. Here are a few cool things I didn't notice about words until I began teaching structured literacy:

- The word barbaric has two identical-looking syllables, but the first one is pronounced "bar" like car and the second one is pronounced "bair".

- The words **discus** and **discuss** have the exact same sounds in both syllables (/d/ /i/ /s/ in the first syllable and /k/ /u/ /s/ in the second syllable) but the two words are not pronounced the same. The only difference between the words is the accenting: DIS-cus, dis-CUSS.

- An accenting difference explains the pronunciation of these two words: local/locale.

- Once Latin roots are understood, they seem to be everywhere! The Latin root *port* means "carry" and can be found in many words: transport, important, report, deport, portly, portfolio, import, export, opportunity, support, deportment, portage, airport, and portable.

- The prefix *co-* means "together", so the word *coincidence* just means that an incident oddly occurred together at the same time as another incident. The word *cooperate* means 'to operate together', with others.

- No more guessing on how to pronounce words like *gapping* vs. *gaping*.

- The letter combination AR represent many different sounds within words, depending on syllable division, whether it's accented or not, whether it's followed by a vowel or a consonant, if the letter W precedes it, if there's a silent e, or if it's part of a vowel team (m**ar**ch w**ar**ning, le**ar**n, **ar**row, **ar**ea, stell**ar**, st**ar**e, liz**ar**d, bo**ar**d, be**ar**, be**ar**d, **ar**ound).

Students *want* to know and understand the logic behind our language, so when they are taught it explicitly, they respond well.

With phonemic awareness and even the most basic of phonics, students begin to realize that written language is not just random strings of letters to be memorized, but information that holds a message. Written text begins to speak to them. Each time a word is accurately decoded, the tasks of reading and spelling become more automatic and fluent. When this happens, it frees up brain power for comprehension, story elements, learning content (like science, social studies , or a new hobby/skill), perspective, analyzing, predicting, questioning, sentence structure, visualizing, grammar, inferring, vocabulary, conventions (capitalization and punctuation), critical thinking, character development, author's point of view, themes, imagination, written expression, and reading for enjoyment.

In the meantime, accommodations (like allowing alternate ways of gaining or showing knowledge, extra time, and the use of audio books) and assistive technology (such as text-to-voice or voice-to-text apps) can and should be utilized. For more information on assistive technology, see *Jamie Martin* in Appendix C.

BONUS SECTION – RELATED

Orthographic Mapping

I have recently learned a great deal from Dr. David Kilpatrick. He realizes the importance of Structured Literacy instruction and knows that reading by decoding creates neural connections that can improve reading fluency.

Here are my main takeaways from his teaching about sight word vocabulary, "orthographic mapping", and the importance of phonemic awareness proficiency.

Sight word vocabulary – a collection of words that are <u>instantly recognized</u>, regardless of regular or irregular spelling and regardless of frequency.

Orthographic lexicon - a collection of words whose correct <u>spelling comes instantly</u> to mind, regardless of regular or irregular spelling and regardless of frequency.

Skilled readers have:

1. the <u>ability to sound out</u> unfamiliar words (whether they learned this on their own or were taught through Structured Literacy).

2. The <u>ability to remember</u> words they read.

   Advanced phonemic skills are needed for both.

Orthographic Mapping – <u>connecting a spoken word to its written form</u> and permanently storing that word in the brain (where it instantly comes to mind, regardless of font, case, cursive, or print). The permanent storage of these words is *not* based on visual skills or visual memory. The permanent storage of these words is orthographic (familiar string of letters), phonologic (sounds), and semantic (meaning). Once a written word is orthographically mapped (remembered/stored), it is never forgotten.

In his books and talks, Dr. Kilpatrick shares the research and theories of Linnea Ehri and David Share.

A part of Linnea Ehri's theory – Segmentation (ability to break apart words into phonemes) and letter-sound skills are central to the connection-forming process (memory).

A piece of David Share's theory – As students sound out words, they are forming orthographic connections. When words are not sounded out, they are poorly remembered. Phonological processing helps remembering.

There is a strong correlation between phonemic awareness skills (learned naturally or taught) and sight word vocabulary.

To give an example of orthographic mapping, I'll use a couple examples of my own.

💜 While sitting and listening to Dr. Kilpatrick, over and over again, I heard him speak of a psychologist "'AIR-y" and her theory. The last name was pronounced just like how the book character Hagrid would say Harry Potter's name: "Arry". It wasn't until much later, after the presentation, when I saw the name *Linnea Ehri* printed in a book that I finally made the connection. Ehri = "Air-y" (a psychologist who has an orthographic mapping theory).

Now, when I hear Dr. Kilpatrick speak of "Ehri", I instantly picture it spelled out in my head, E-h-r-i. And when I see the name *Ehri* printed on a page, it automatically pops into my mind, pronounced as "AIR-ee".

💜 One of my 6th grade students correctly read the word *nod*. Since she said it hesitantly, I explained and demonstrated, "Like you're nodding your head."

She immediately came back with, "Or like you're gnawing on something." By sound, the words *nod* and *gnawed* are the same! The girl had an amazing vocabulary and had definitely heard the word *nod* before, but she had not yet mapped this word orthographically, meaning she had not yet connected the meaning of the word *nod* with its spelling.

💜 When I was teaching 6th grade, I read aloud to my students every day. One of the most enjoyable books to read was the first Harry Potter book and it had just been published (no movies yet). When I got to one of the main character's names, Hermione, I had no clue how to pronounce it. My 6th graders and I made guesses: Her-me-won? Her-me-own? We decided to just nickname the character "Hermy" (HER-mee) and that's what I would say when I got to her name. Until.... someone online gave a hint at how to pronounce it. The person suggested saying the three words "Her", "My" and "Knee" all together. After a few times, I was able to then recognize and remember Hermione as "Her-my-nee".

Orthographic mapping occurs in the brains of people who understand the connection between sounds and letters. Essentially, once a person has read a word by sounding it out or decoding it, then the next time the word is encountered, it is easier to decode. When this has happened enough times for the brain to be able to automatically read a word, then the printed word and the spoken word are connected or "mapped". Orthographic mapping works for names, regular and irregularly spelled words, and even symbols.

If you know the code (think periodic table of elements), you may be able to figure out the coded message on these license plates. The more times you decipher a code, the more easily its message pops out at you. If you do not know the code, then the message will remain hidden to you:

For more on orthographic mapping and phonemic proficiency, see **Dr. David Kilpatrick** in Appendix C.

Do the eyes look at and process all the letters?

Although it appears automatic when the brain becomes efficient at reading, the eyes DO look at and process each and every letter in words. I know there are shortcuts to text-language (like LOL) and some people take advantage of predictive text options, but even when teenagers spell out all the letters of words, it appears as though their thumbs are just flying over the phone's keyboard and that the text messages are magically appearing, whole words or sentences at a time.

Does this mean that their thumbs don't have to stop on each individual letter? No, their thumbs DO have to touch each letter, but because their brains have learned the exact thumb movement needed for most words, it can seem that words are appearing as whole words rather than as a letter at a time.

The same is true when typing on a computer keyboard. With practice and repetition, there are certain words that can be typed out automatically, quickly, and without looking. For me, my name is one of those "automatic" words. Since I can type it in a split second, it appears as though I am not touching the individual letter keys of my name and that it shows up automatically. I get proof that my fingers much touch each individual key when my fingers are not lined up right and are scooched over just one position to the right; my brain still follows the learned finger movement pattern and I end up with "Larom" rather than "Karin".

A person texting (or typing) a new word or a person new to texting will show slow and deliberate touching of each letter, starting with the first letter and moving to the next:

peck......peck........ peck. With each successful texting of a word, the act of texting becomes more and more fluent. Although each letter must still be touched, texting begins to appear automatic.

A person reading a new word or a person new to reading will be slow and deliberate. The reader will have to slow down, and the eyes have to pay attention to each little piece of the word starting on the left and moving to the right: /k/... /e/... /p/ ... /t/. With each successful reading of a word, the act of reading becomes more and more fluent. Although each individual letter and word-part must still be looked at and processed from left to right, reading begins to appear automatic.

If a student has not been taught to look at the letters from right to left, then chances are pretty good that they ARE looking at the middle of the word and seeing it as a whole picture/shape, in which case they will continue to confuse words like expect/except, destiny/density, Calvary/Cavalry, reverence/relevance, sacred/scared/scarred/scarce, Cindy/Sydney, reverse/reserve, girl/grill, own/now/won, form/from, preform/perform, and clam/calm.

BONUS SECTION - STORIES

Top Ten Ways to Become a Better Reader

Before I knew about dyslexia and Structured Literacy instruction, I put huge effort into getting kids to love books and motivating them to practice reading as much as possible.

I amassed a very large collection of my own personal books for students to check out daily, met kids in the school library to help point out good book choices, read the backs of books to pique interest, read aloud using good expression and character voices, and dressed up for all the book-related spirit days like "Read Across America Day" and "Dress as a Book Character Day". I encouraged students to read over the summer and even created a "Summer Reading Challenge" that rewarded students with lemonade, Rice Krispie treats and play-time at a local park.

One year, when I was a small-group reading teacher, I remember designing a bulletin board based off of a Scholastic Book Clubs bookmark that said, "Top 10 Ways to Become a Better Reader". On the bulletin board, I drew a person snorkeling while reading a book. I took various pictures of students demonstrating all ten ways listed on the bookmark and displayed the student pictures on the bulletin board. According to the bookmark, here are the top 10 ways to become a better reader:

1. Read
2. Read
3. Read
4. Read
5. Read
6. Read
7. Read
8. Read
9. Read
10. Read

I had fun creating the bulletin board. One student was pictured reading a book while going down a slide. Others posed on top of the jungle gym, hanging upside down on the monkey bars, or snuggled into a comfy chair, all while holding an open book.

After describing the bulletin board to my mom, she said, "I don't get it. What am I missing?"

I explained to her the philosophy behind the "best way to become a better reader is to read" idea: The more time that kids spend reading, the better they get at reading. Kind of a "practice makes perfect" philosophy.

I did succeed at getting kids to read at home and I do believe that I succeeded at getting kids to love books and stories, but I was missing a key piece.

Don't get me wrong here: A love of books and reading at home are both good things! All the things I did were wonderful and really did succeed in getting kids to love stories, but I now know that students need to know how to effectively and accurately read by decoding (whether their brains figure it out themselves or they are taught) before reading every night will make them better readers.

The Rug, Carpet, Mat Story
(This is probably the story that I have shared the most with parents and educators)

Before I knew about dyslexia and before I knew about phonemic awareness and its importance, I was teaching a small group of 1st graders. While meeting one-on-one with a 1st grade student, I asked her to read a teeny tiny "book" to me. It wasn't actually a book; it was just a single sheet of paper folded into fourths. It wasn't actually a story; it just contained a few phrases for the student to read in order to learn the commonly used word, "**a**". The book in its entirety contained eight words, grouped into two-word phrases, each with a picture above it. One of the phrases read, *a mat*. Above it was a cat, curled up and sleeping on a welcome mat. The girl started off "reading" the book just fine, pointing to each word and saying each one correctly: "a seed... a cat.... a flower...".

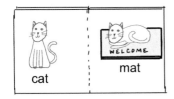

When she got to the *mat* part of the little book, she read, "a rug".

I wasn't too surprised at her mistake, knowing that she had relied on the picture to make her guess, but I prompted, "Look at the first letter."

"Oh," she shook her head, "I mean *carpet*."

Even more baffled now, I pointed to the **m** in *mat* and asked, "What sound does this letter make?"

"MMM," she correctly replied.

"How about this one?" I asked, pointing to the **a** in *mat*.

"/aaah/" she correctly replied.

"And this one?" I asked, pointing to the letter **t** in *mat*.

Again, she responded with the correct sound, "/t/".

I was confident that she could now blend those sounds together to get "mat" and I even reinforced the process for her by repeating the sounds back to her: "mmmm...aaaaaa...t". Not only was she *still* not able to read the word mat, she was looking at me like I was bonkers. She had no idea in the world what I was doing. She tried her original guesses of "rug" and "carpet" and then looked at me for help. Exasperated, I finally just told her that the word was "mat" and introduced it into her vocabulary by giving her a few examples.

In hindsight, this experience taught me a great deal:

- Students can *appear* to be reading when they may actually have memorized the words in the book. Although this student said, "a flower" in just the right spot, if I had written the word *flower* on a separate piece of paper and shown it to her, I'm fairly certain that she would not have been able to read it.

- A student can know phonics (the sounds that letters make/say/represent) and still not know how to use phonics to read.

- While pictures in a book are entertaining and can assist students in imagining the story in their heads, relying on the pictures in order to read the words is **not** an effective strategy.

- Students need phonemic awareness before letter/sound correspondences and reading-by-decoding will make sense.

- If not taught about it in their teacher training, even experienced teachers can be blind to dyslexia.

Slow and Steady (with the right kind of instruction) Wins the Race

B.M. began with me before his 8th grade year. According to his parents, he did not begin talking until he was 4 years old. He had already been held back a grade, had been in speech therapy, and had been in special education classes since Kindergarten.

When I met him as a 14-year-old, he was unable to read even the most decodable 1st-grade-level words and here is a picture of his attempt at writing the sentence, "The quick brown fox jumped over the lazy dogs."

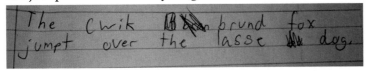

The special education team at his middle school had just told his parents that they had tried all they could and they didn't know what else to do.

B.M was one of the most profoundly dyslexic students I have ever worked with. When he began with me, he had no knowledge of the difference between a letter and a sound, had no phonemic awareness, could not pronounce "spaghetti", and had strong confusion of letters like b/d/p and n/u.

He took longer than my other students to complete each lesson, but he began to see the value and success of the lessons and was determined to learn to read.

Our first year, I was correcting errors such as act/ask, bog/dog, fist/first and camp/cap. His first attempt at reading the irregular word *said* was "sighed" and then he changed his guess to "sad". He struggled through stories with words like *Sam, yum,* and *blind.*

Our fourth year, I was still correcting errors, but they were with words like silence/stillness, insistent/incident, and overreacted/overcorrected. He was learning irregular words like *nuisance, disease,* and *ancient.* He. still struggled through the reading of stories, but now with words like *controversial, obstinate, infuriated, and beneficial.*

B.M. worked SO hard. He even drove to my house for a lesson when school had been cancelled due to snow.

During his fifth year of structured literacy instruction, I got a text from B.M. that included a picture that he had taken of his computer screen at school, showing a graph of his progression on a school reading test that is used to determine if a remedial reading class is needed or not. Students need 1000 points in order to get out of the reading class and be freed up to take an elective.

The attached graph includes neither the beginning nor the end of our five years of lessons, but it does show the tremendous reading growth that occurred in the middle. If you can't read the numbers on the graph, the first score (213) was from 9/9/13. The last score (1040) was from 3/17/15.

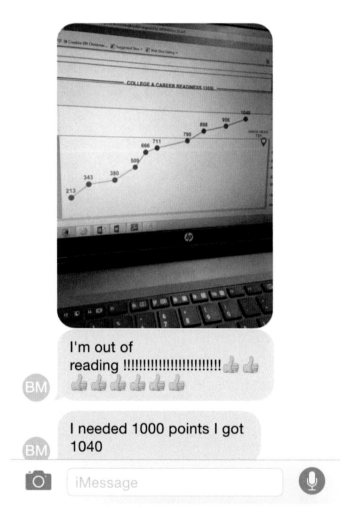

The moral of this story is two-fold:

1. It would have been better for B.M. to get the right kind of reading instruction when he was younger, but this story and graph show that it is never too late to learn to read.

2. Although B.M.'s teachers and special educators had big hearts and tried everything they knew to help him, they did not know about dyslexia and they were not aware of the teaching method needed to help him.

I finally understand WHY…

In Kindergarten, H.G. was given a worksheet. Students were to circle the picture that "didn't belong". The actual task was to find the picture whose first sound/letter was different than that of the other pictures. The pictures included a bat, a bee, and a cat. Henry circled the bee, indicating that it didn't belong with the bat and the cat since it was the only picture that was not a mammal.

After two years of structured literacy, H.G. scored "Advanced" on the state standardized test. Here are a few reflections about his years before structured literacy:

> "In 4th grade, I had to read *Farmer Boy*. It was the worst experience of my entire life. I had so much trouble reading it. The words seemed not to be right. It was like trying to read ancient text that had been lost for centuries and I didn't know the root language."

> Getting emotional and teary-eyed as he thought back, he remembered, "Even words I thought I knew how to read, I didn't."

> Speaking about the challenge of thinking, composing, and actually writing all at the same time he explained, "As I went through school, I just struggled and struggled with reading and writing assignments. I was told I just needed to pick up and stop slacking off. But I worked as hard as I could. I've got a bajillion-track mind. With some things, I just run out of tracks. I was always like, 'I know this! Why can't I get this?! I would know the topic but just couldn't put it down into words.' It's easier to check now, though. Sometimes I just get hasty when I'm writing and then I forget."

"I finally understand WHY I wasn't normal. I wasn't just stupid. I wasn't just not trying hard enough. I had dyslexia. Everyone else is 2-dimensional. I am 3-dimensional. Therefore, I work differently. I see things differently and I think about things differently and I'm in a different dimension."

Adults

Common in stories of adults are these comments:

- "I knew something was wrong."
- "I thought I had *something*."
- "I knew I was different."
- "I worked extremely hard."

Many of them didn't learn about their own dyslexia until one of their own kids started to struggle with language tasks.

To order a DVD featuring many of the adults mentioned in this book (H.G., D.L., R.B., M.H., G.M., K.C., and J.H.), see Appendix A.

D.L. - Attorney

"I knew the minute I went to school I was different than the other kids. We used to sit around in a circle, and the teacher would have flash cards. The other kids were getting the answers, and I wouldn't. And man, I couldn't figure that out because I knew I was as smart as those other kids, but I couldn't get it."

"I never learned how to read by the letters. But I did learn to read by syllable and shape. And I'm also what's called an "intuitive reader", meaning that by my knowledge of what goes on in the world and how people talk and history and everything else, I can figure out where the story's going."

"I never could spell, and can't spell to this day."

"When I graduated from law school, I was one of the top students in the class. But the secret never went away and at the time I went to law school, they were actually having litigation over whether dyslexic people could go to law school. And I certainly never told the law school admission committee that I was dyslexic."

"I was fortunate: The way dyslexia manifested itself in me makes me very good at putting together complex facts patterns and finding the simple storyline through the middle of it. And that's basically what you have to do in law school. You have to take all of this stuff and put it together in a coherent solution to the problem that you are faced with."

R.B. – Physician and Health Clinic Owner

R.B. didn't have the normal struggles caused by his dyslexia until Medical School. "I excelled really, in school and college, but I think a lot of that was because I worked extremely hard. I was very much a visual learner. I never missed a class, because that's really how I learned. I couldn't sit down with a book and pore over it two or three times and really get out the information that I needed. My struggles really came with the career that I chose. At times, I felt like I was cursed. Because my dad was very ill when I was growing up and I remember I was the youngest of five children. I was old enough that you couldn't leave me at home; but yet, you wouldn't get a babysitter, so I went to the doctor's office a lot with my dad. That really made an impression on me; what that career did for my family. And so, at a very young age, 7th, 8th grade, I knew I wanted to be a doctor. So, it was just a matter of being able to achieve all of the hurdles to become that career."

"The first year of medical school was not really that difficult for me because the first year is a lot of visual learning and that was my way of learning. The second year was very, very difficult for me and my problems started to show up. In second year, they would not lecture on all the material. You'd have to do a lot of reading. For instance, in Pathology, which was in your second year, they may lecture for three or four hours but then you may have to read another 100 to 200 pages that they never lectured on but yet they'd test over. I thought to myself, 'How can I read all this?!' I was such a slow reader that I didn't have the time to be able to know my notes that I'd taken all day in class and be able to read the extra pages. There were also multiple-choice standardized tests. And there would be hundreds and hundreds of questions. My problem was *not* that I didn't know the material. I just didn't read fast enough to get through all the questions, so a lot of times I would leave a third or more of my test unanswered."

"My struggles brought out that work ethic in me and I was able to achieve."

<u>B.L. – Land Surveyor and Professional Photographer</u>
Always very creative and good at visualization, B.L. knew he was different for a long time. "I would spend five or six hours on homework and still not be done. The more I got into school, the more trouble I got into."

Just thinking back to small-group read aloud time gave B.L. a lot of anxiety.

On an untimed Otis-Lennon test that measures critical thinking, reasoning skills, speed of thought, and ability to see relationships and patterns, B.L. scored so well that people thought he was slacking off on other tests and tasks. "You're obviously not applying yourself," they'd say.

When it came to the Standardized Achievement Test (SAT), B.L. would run out of time to complete the test and would resort to "just filling in the bubbles", but when he took land surveying exams, he would have extra time left over, due to knowledge gained through hands-on experience and *listening* to land surveying books.

After a counselor told him he was "better suited to garbage collector," B.L. went on to attend college where he received training in a variety of fields such as law and architecture., ultimately deciding to follow his strengths and passion of photography and land surveying.

M.H. – Educator and Child Advocate

"I really was an amazing actor and an expert at memorization," M.H. said of not being able to read until college. "None of my teachers knew."

"What allowed me to fake it so successfully was my parents bought all of the textbooks from the district every year. And then, my father and I would stay up at night and memorize. He would read it out loud to me and I would regurgitate it verbatim. And we would do this every night. Then I would go to school and they would call on me, and I would recite what it was by memory and kind of move my finger around like everybody else did."

In college, one of her professors tested her for dyslexia and taught her how to deal with "cracking the code" of written language. She relates language to a chemistry equation: "Just like chemistry, hydrogen or all of the elements and they all interact differently with one another and when you put them together you have this beautiful equation. But behind those letters [element symbols] are molecules and all of these different things that interact with one another. For me, that is how I see language."

I think the biggest hurdle for me was to understand that my stubbornness was a strength and that to conquer learning and to excel in my own life and what I wanted for myself, was to become a fighter and not give up. Once I wrapped my head around the fact that my stubbornness was a strength and that I needed to utilize every strategy possible, then I excelled.

M.H. has earned two Master's Degrees, one of which is a Master's Degree in Reading for which she did her thesis on **reading**. Of the thesis and the degree, M.H. explained, "I only did that because I wanted to prove to myself and everyone else that I do know how to read. There's that stubbornness."

"My advice to anyone who has a child, or yourself, who may be feeling the struggle or the heartache of trying to crack the code of dyslexia, is to have a real firm inner fire. That knowing that the finish line is in sight and that when you have this strength of stubbornness, it is guaranteed that you will get to the finish line. We'll all be here cheering you on when you reach it."

G.M. – Deputy Base Civil Engineer

"I knew I was different very early on, but it didn't bother me that much. I did figure out that I couldn't spell. And I remember in grade school, every time there was a spelling test, I'd tell my teacher I was sick and she would let me put my head down."

"I couldn't read out loud at all. I would be so nervous and embarrassed, so most teachers just realized I couldn't read out loud and let me skip through that."

G.M. did not speak full sentences until age 6 and would do a lot of grunting and pointing. Being very late to talk, going through a lot of speech therapy, and having trouble reading and spelling, other parents assumed that G.M. had mental difficulties. One family even wanted to know if G.M might want to join their son in attending a "special school" the following year.

"In high school, teachers suggested that I use a dictionary to help with spelling. I would tell them, 'I can't use a dictionary because I don't even know what the word starts with!' I can't put letters and sounds together at all."

From early on, G.M.'s parents owned a farm and business and the whole family worked hard, from sunrise to sunset. G.M. credits the good work ethic instilled in him for helping him get through life and helping him excel in his job, by just working harder than everybody else does. G.M.'s parents recognized him as a hard worker, kind to others, an inventor, always taking things apart, and as "an entrepreneur from the get-go." G.M. is a good decision-maker and can "see" the solution to 3D puzzles. Everyone liked G.M. and he was a superb negotiator. He built relationships with people around him, was good at networking, and he had a great attitude, saying, "I had teachers who would ignore my spelling because I had such a good attitude. They knew what I was trying to write and they would just grade me on my thought pattern rather than my spelling and punctuation."

First discouraged and depressed at having an engineering degree and yet just pumping gas, G.M. kept working hard. Through good attitude and grit, G.M. went from having high self-doubt to having confidence in himself: "I can do anything I put my mind to."

By working hard and doing his best, G.M. climbed the ladder to Deputy Base Civil Engineer at Ellsworth Air Force Base and likened it to taking care of and maintaining a small town.

G.M.'s advice to young people:

- Learn.

- Apply for jobs.

- Take classes.

- Take certifications.

- Make yourself available.

- Have a good attitude. Toward your bosses, your teachers, and anybody you work for.

- Never worry about your next job. Don't worry about your next grade. Just do your very best at the job you're in and you'll succeed.

As an adult, G.M. now reads every night. "I'm a very slow reader, but I have fallen in love with the mental picture you get from reading."

K.C. – Lieutenant Commander in the US Public Health Service, Dietician

"I knew as a youngster that my brain was wired differently. I didn't have a word for it, I just knew that I had to learn to compensate. I always had to apply myself more and allow more time. I always built that extra time in there, like in college I spent much more time in the library than my classmates, because I knew that I *had* to, to succeed.

When her grades dropped and she was kicked out of an accelerated program, it was a blow to her self-esteem and she cried a lot. One person even wrote her a letter, suggesting that she was better suited for a job in the Post Office. "There will always be people who don't believe in you," K.C. noted, but she refused to give up. She decided to set high expectations, persevere, and believe in herself.

"I couldn't take the 17 or 18-credit load and maintain any kind of grade point average," K.C. realized, "so I would take fewer courses and take my toughest courses in the summer."

For example, when she was failing Organic Chemistry, she would stay hyper-focused to soak up as much learning as possible, and then drop the class on the last drop date and take the course again the following semester. By doing this for six semesters and by utilizing summer school, she got through Organic Chemistry and was able to maintain A's and B's in college.

K.C.'s own struggles and experiences with dyslexia grew into a strength in her profession as a dietician. Her patients at Indian Health Services value her educational approach and cultural examples. K.C. shared, "Sometimes I think have advantages over other dieticians because the way I communicate with my patients, and the way I teach them. I think their ability to learn from me is sometimes even heightened, because I use certain tricks, and pictures, and visuals, and things like that. That really gets through to my patients and helps them to really understand.

K.C.'s advice:

- Apply yourself. - "I'm not afraid to put in the hard work to achieve what might be easier for another person, but you can get there too."

- Don't let the failures define you.

- Focus on and nurture strengths and talents. – K.C.'s talents included tennis, cross-country skiing, and modeling. "I think one thing that really, really helped me was the islands of excellence that keep your confidence and ego strong. And you really, really need that."

- Life is not a race. Set goals and do what it takes.

K.C. was instrumental in modifying the outdated Food Pyramid into "My Plate" which better reflects Native American health knowledge and balance. A circle divided into 4ths (an important symbol in many native cultures) is incorporated into the design. Using nutritional information and historical health patterns, K.C. teaches about nutrition and diabetes prevention.

J.H. – Navy/Marine Corps, VA Health Care Administrator (retired)

"In elementary school, I couldn't read, write, or spell. I became pretty good at math and geography and those were my islands of excellence."

His small parochial school provided discipline, predictability, and structure, an environment where J.H. was able to develop coping skills.

His mom, a teacher, showed compassion, understanding, and love. As long as he gave it his best in school, she only required an A in Deportment (behavior). "Don't worry about your spelling," she would say. "You'll have a secretary or assistant someday to do your writing for you." Other advice and encouragement from his mom included, "Focus on what you CAN do, not on what you can't do."

J.H. graduated with multiple degrees: Chemistry, Psychology, Biochemical Pharmacology, and Healthcare Administration.

While in the Marine Corps, J.H. recalls someone incredulously asking him, "You have a college degree! How could you misspell *'rifle'*?!"

J.H. sees himself and other dyslexics as out-of-the-box thinkers versus linear thinkers and thinks that people who see in images (in their brains) rather than in words get a bigger picture of the world. And, since people with dyslexia are often great with patterns, J.H. would teach the members of his Naval Intelligence team to "think like a dyslexic" when solving cases or breaking codes.

Advice from J.H.

- Delegate, which gives you the chance to think/plan/be strategic.

- Learn to be tenacious.

- Get back up and go at it from a different angle.

- Never give up.

J.H. believes that techniques, strategies, and instruction that work for people with dyslexia are techniques, strategies, and instruction that work for *everyone*. He relays an analogy from an image of students waiting for the stairs to be shoveled before being able to enter their school. A student in a wheelchair astutely points out, "If you shovel the ramp, we can ALL go in."

Now J.H has used his own experiences with dyslexia to help write a state handbook for dyslexia and to be a role model and tireless advocate for students with dyslexia and other learning differences.

Z.V. - Incredible Insight into Hindsight
Just like dyslexia can sometimes mask intelligence, intelligence can sometimes mask dyslexia.

Z.V., a young adult at the time of the interview, found it interesting to look back at his childhood, with hindsight.

His mom, a teacher, had taken child development very seriously and "did an incredible job" with raising him. She read to Z.V. every single night. As he grew older and his mom encouraged him to start reading to her, Z.V. recalled "I was very excited and I wanted to, very much." Finding reading aloud difficult, Z.V. always found a way to "weasel out of it" by bargaining with his mom so that he only had to read a line or two and then she would read the rest.

Z.V. was always very curious. When learning about a new subject or topic, he would press his mom for more information. "I wanted specific, in-depth knowledge on all the topics I asked about, and I was not satisfied until I had it," he recalled. "I had to know everything about it." His mom continued to read to him and she purchased a set of encyclopedias from which to pull information and answers to share with Z.V.

This daily routine at home led to a very broad knowledge base, which helped Z.V. compensate during all of his schooling. When the class would cover a topic that he already knew and testing on the topic began, teachers would be very impressed, likely thinking, "Wow, Z.V. picks up everything we teach him!" and "He must really be reading!"

"When in fact," Z.V. explained, "it was just stuff that was *told* to me outside of school and I soaked it up."

Knowing what he knows now about dyslexia Z.V. looks back and realizes that there were signs in his writing and spelling that "clearly showed a kid with dyslexia," but his intelligence and knowledge masked his struggle with reading, so the signs were missed.

When the reading material became longer and more complex, Z.V. remembers it being very difficult.

Of his reading homework, he recalled, "I would spend *hours* reading. I would practice it over and over and focus *so* hard,". When it was Z.V.'s turn to read aloud in class the next day, it sounded choppy and full of mistakes. The teacher told him, "You've obviously never read it." Frustrated at how hard he had worked on the passage the previous night, but not wanting to reveal to his peers his inability to read, Z.V. did not protest.

As he tried again and again, with little improvement, Z.V. began to realize that he wasn't getting much from the reading assignments anyway. How could he comprehend and learn from the text when so much of his focus and energy was spent trying to decode it?

One evening, Z.V. decided to not spend any time on the reading homework. The following day, his teacher's response was identical: "You've obviously never read it."

Z.V. learned from that experience that his teacher's reaction and his grade would be the same, regardless of the time and energy he spent. He reasoned, "If working hard elicits the same response as not working hard, why work hard?" So, he stopped working hard and gave up trying to read his textbooks.

Although Z.V. stopped reading, he didn't stop learning. He would pick up information from any source that he could. If the class was learning about farming, he would talk to his grandpa, a farmer. He would search out and talk to adults with experience on the topic or listen to his mom read and teach from the set of encyclopedias. Although the teachers may have noticed in Z.V.'s homework, reports, and tests that the information was different than that presented by the textbook, they couldn't argue that Z.V. had solid facts and insight and often held a deeper understanding of a topic than his classmates.

"I always figured out different ways of doing things. They would teach us one method or one technique and I'd find it hard, so I would just dissect it and develop a different technique. Particularly in math I did this a lot. I could get the answer by working it out in my head, using some short cuts I had worked out."

Although he was excited for his first computer class in 6th grade, Z.V. hit his first real wall when his class began to learn to type. "They would put a book on an easel, place a piece of paper over our hands, and then we'd play the word typing game. I was terrible! Everything was backwards and mixed up!"

Z.V. had learned to do a lot of things in school by finding and then memorizing patterns. Typing was no different. He tried to learn each word's pattern of finger movement on the keyboard, but lamented, "My head wasn't grasping it. Everything was flip-flopped and reversed."

Seeing his typing, a teacher made a comment: "Maybe you're dyslexic or something."

It was the first time Z.V. had heard the word *dyslexia*. Not knowing what it meant, he asked his mom. She didn't know much about dyslexia at the time. They decided together that Z.V. couldn't *possibly* have dyslexia since he was raised with the premise of "there's nothing wrong with you", he was getting good reading grades, he was an excellent learner, and he didn't write things upside down. The idea of dyslexia was dismissed.

To help survive in middle school when he began to really have trouble, Z.V. became friends with all the teachers. He reasoned, "It's hard to fail or give a bad grade to a student you're friends with. Someone who comes in while everyone else is out there playing and wants to ask you about the assignment, wants to learn more, and asks for extra credit."

Z.V. said that what was incredible about his "really amazing" teachers wasn't necessarily their teaching technique, but how much they cared for him and were interested in him as a person. They were accepting and encouraging.

In middle school, Z.V. ventured into music and found it to be a good outlet. Without ever learning to read sheet music, he learned to play percussion instruments like the drum, xylophone, and vibraphone by finding and then memorizing the patterns of each song. To do this, he would start by labeling every single note on every page of sheet music. Then he would label the instrument with pieces of masking tape and start working out the patterns. In this way, he would memorize the patterns of notes and movements of a six to eight-page piece of music and eventually be able to play the whole song with his eyes on the conductor, never having to look at the instrument or the music. Z.V. did this for many, many songs. As painstaking and incredible as the process was, he found it much easier than trying to read the sheet music.

The more Z.V. treated music as a focus area, the more he began to excel at it. And once he found the musician within himself, this gave him a little bit of an *identity*. Being known as "the kid who was doing college-level music" took the pressure off of other school-related stresses and allowed Z.V. to get excused from things like an extra study hall period.

Leaving behind the rapport he had built with middle-school teachers and entering into a whole different dynamic, Z.V. found high school to be "really rough". His memory of the ordeal is heart-breaking:

"Still not knowing what's going on in your head really beats you up. It brings down your self-esteem and brings you pretty low. It was really hard. Very rough. I found out that I could not excel in school like I had thought. When I was young, I had desire and drive. At 10 years old, I wanted to have a doctorate degree by 28 [years old] and I was excited for life. That drive went away. Entirely."

"School wasn't important anymore."

"School went downhill really quick. No one understood. Here was this kid who was on the Knowledge Bowl Team and who was in the Talented and Gifted program, but here he was, essentially failing classes. The only reason I didn't fail is that some of the teachers would give me a break or ... I don't even know how I passed some of them. I never did homework. Ever."

"I didn't care anymore. I didn't have any real direction for life, for a career. No idea what to focus on or think about. No drive."

When the hormones of the teenage years hit, Z.V.'s ADD went into overtime and life became very stressful. "It was insane," he recalled. Working with the special education department was "an absolute disaster", he was fighting with his mom, music was his only outlet, and he still had no idea what was going on. His mom could tell that he was depressed.

Z.V. began a transformation into punk rock. He wore "weird clothes" (his words), spiked, colored hair, mohawks, and gauges (stretched out holes in the earlobes). Although Z.V. never did drugs, never did drink, and had never been in trouble with the law, his mom contacted a Juvenile Diversion program coordinator when he began leaving home often. Although he was never technically "running away from home" since he would always return by nighttime, he *was* running away from his problems and from conversations with his mom.

In meeting with the diversion officer, Z.V. was pleasantly surprised that, unlike with previous therapists and counselors, the focus was not on his green spiky hair or his clothing. The focus was not on his outward appearance at all. The officer was simply sitting there, interested in Z.V. the person and genuinely wanting to get to know him. This led to an agreement by Z.V. to return for more conversations, which covered Z.V.'s interests, music styles, and then eventually topics of school. "Maybe I have dyslexia," Z.V. flippantly mused, recalling his keyboarding teacher's words, but then reasoned it away due to his misconceptions of dyslexia: "I'm not trying to toot my own horn," he explained, "but I'm *smart*."

Meetings with the diversion officer continued, but so did the struggles in school. Growing increasingly worried, Z.V.'s mom began to look into the possibility of sending Zane to a live-in home for troubled boys.

One night, having given up hope and frustrated with life, failing high school and his mom minutes way from calling the Boys Home, Z.V.'s mom made one last-ditch effort and called someone suggested earlier by the diversion officer. That someone was J.H., the mentor and advocate described in the previous story.

Z.V.'s first reaction about the call was, "This is dumb. No, I'm not going to try another scheme." but when his mom held the phone out to Zane with J.H. waiting on the other end, he reluctantly lifted the phone to his ear.

The phone call led to face-to-face conversations and a friendship that would change the trajectory of his life.

J.H. was a Naval and Marine Corps veteran retired from multiple careers, who happened to have dyslexia himself. While talking to J.H. and answering questions from a dyslexia screening, Z.V. began to realize the reason for his struggles: he perfectly fit the profile of a person with dyslexia.

More importantly, Z.V. saw in J.H. a highly intelligent, well-respected and well-achieved person, telling his *own* tale of dyslexia. The two were both intelligent and similar in many ways. He had finally met someone with whom he could relate. Z.V. found J.H. positive and full of energy, his stories fascinating and intriguing. Z.V. felt honored to be around him and was happy to have "someone in his corner".

J.H. saw the potential in Z.V. and took him under his wing and began to mentor him. He taught helpful organizational and advocacy skills and took him to dyslexia conferences where he "met people from all over the world, all very achieved and saying they went through the same damn thing in school." J.H. helped Z.V. make connections with business owners where he gained insight on how to run a successful business.

Z.V.'s work ethic and drive returned, and not only did he finish high school, but his grades improved and he was able to graduate a year early.

In college at the time of my interview, Z.V. reflected back:

"I was forced to have to do more than the average to have a better understanding. That and everything that I've learned as a coping mechanism or through my strange way of doing things gives me an advantage over a lot of things."

"Being aware of dyslexia has helped in college. I get help when I need it, and I'm respected as an out-of-the-box thinker and puzzle-solver."

"In discussions and brainstorming sessions, I normally come up with at least one different angle than everyone else comes up with. It's neat to have a different, outside, nonstandard thought."

"One of the skills that I value the most in me is probably my ability to problem-solve. In anything. In math, in puzzles, in providing a solution to a need, in life."

In looking to the future, Z.V. knows he will be diverse with what he ends up doing. He wants to create, build, and run successful businesses. With his drive back on track and with the grit and perseverance he gained through his experiences with dyslexia, Z.V. will go far.

ABOUT THE AUTHOR

Rapid City Dyslexia Care
Posted by Karin Merkle
October 7, 2015 ·

My top wish for people with dyslexia is surprisingly not the wish that they would be better readers or spellers (although that is possible with the right kind of teaching). My top wish for people with dyslexia is that teachers and society would view them with awe and wonder and jealousy for their strengths and potential strengths. Seriously, I hope someday people say, "You have dyslexia? Wow, you're lucky!"

After teaching in the public schools for almost twenty years in a variety of settings including whole-class, small group, and one-on-one, Karin started her own private tutoring business to give specialized reading and spelling lessons to adults and children with dyslexia.

Living in the Black Hills of South Dakota, Karin strives to raise awareness of dyslexia and the need for structured literacy instruction.

More by Karin:

- ♥ Article on dyslexia, **"Good News about Bright Children Who Struggle with Reading and Spelling"**, published in EP Magazine's Annual Education Issue in September 2014 as "A New Perspective".

- ♥ **"Teacher Heads-up packet"**, with quick information and resources about dyslexia and some common ways for teachers to support students with dyslexia in their classrooms.

- ♥ **DVD** of panel guests of adults with dyslexia, sharing their experiences and advice (best paired with the documentary The Big Picture: Rethinking Dyslexia).

- ♥ **Razor the Resolute**, a mascot of all-things-dyslexia, who gives encouragement to students, parents, and professionals to "hang in there" even when things are difficult.

God's Word (Jesus) gives light, love, life, and hope. True peace can be found through the Word for those who seek it.

APPENDIX A –Videos, Images

To learn more and hear directly from many of the adults mentioned in this book (H.G., D.L., R.B., M.H., G.M., K.C., and J.H.), you can order a DVD in which you can watch them during a panel discussion about dyslexia.

To view the following videos, go to the "Videos" tab of rcdyslexiacare.com or email rcdyslexiacare@gmail.com for a digital copy of this page so you can click on the hyperlinks and go straight to each video:

- Hand-made goat chute rigged with spring-loaded door (59-second video)
- Three Cubes? (3-minute video) - This student's creation and perception is the reason for the hexagon (or cube) on the cover of this book. Below is the visual hint:

  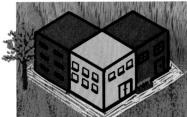

  *For another very cool optical/perception demonstration, search online for paper trays optical illusion.
- Letter Formation, lowercase p (7-second video)
- Letter Formation, lowercase g (16-second video)
- Letter Formation, lowercase e (21-second video)
- Letter Formation, lowercase r (13 second video)
- Letter Formation, lowercase r (1-minute video)
- Letter Formation, lowercase n (48-second video)
- Pencil Grip (18-second video)
- Little Square/Big Square, geometric tile creation (27-second video)
- Advice from a student, and an example of up/down confusion (3-minute video)
- Dyslexia and is there a right or wrong way to make a star? (3 ½-minute video)

APPENDIX B – For Fun

This page may help to reinforce that the confusion and errors of dyslexia are not due to "seeing things backwards" at all. The activities on this page illustrate why certain tasks are tricky for people with dyslexia, but they are also just fun ways to get your brain thinking, seeing, and perceiving.

Can a star be backwards?

Apparently, if you eat a donut with the frosting-side down, the sweet taste of the frosting hits your taste buds more quickly and is delicious, but how many of you would look at someone eating a donut that way as eating it "upside-down"? Here are some other things that seem backwards or upside down when it doesn't **really** matter: cookie, slice of pizza, getting an envelope with the opening flap on bottom.

A dollar bill is $1.00 no matter which way it's facing, but there actually is a correct way to lay the bills in a cash register. For the bank machines to "read" and count them, they must be face-up and the top of the head of the person featured on the bill should be toward the right. This seems silly, but once you learn the "correct way", bills in other directions feel backwards and will likely bother you.

Can a heart shape be "backwards"? You can test it out by writing it on a clear transparent sheet or on a window. Viewing from the inside or outside of the window yields the same shape.

How about a star? To see an interesting video in which a student draws a star and I talk about it, see "Can a star be backwards?" in Appendix A.

Two overlapping triangles   Two overlapping cursors

How about a smiley face?

How do you make a check mark?

Imagine the waving guy from page 28.  Is he waving hello and looking at you? Are you sure? This image works as both a "Hello" and a "Goodbye" message, depending on your perspective (whether you are walking *into* the store or *out of* the store). Let's pretend that he is indeed looking at you. Would you agree, then, that ⥾𝒪 would be a good symbol for "Hello"? Alternately, 𝒪⥾ would be the symbol for "Goodbye". Even with frequent practice walking in and out of the store and seeing the image daily, will you remember which is which?

⥾𝒪
represents "Hello"

𝒪⥾
represents "Goodbye"

Below are some of the examples of confusion and errors are related to perception and viewpoint that I listed earlier in the book. None of the examples involve reading, writing, or spelling, but try to imagine that they do. Draw a few of them on your transparency sheet or your window to help imagine:

- looking at a clock with hands (is that 3:00 or 9:00?)
- reading a map
- distinguishing between "before" or "after"
- writing the letter b or d
- using greater than or less than symbols (> <)

Some words and numbers are the same from either direction. Have fun experimenting with other drawings, like an animal, words like *wow*, *mom*, and *I*, certain letters or numbers like *u, n, b, A, d, 25, 52.*

This fun experiment is why I chose 02-02-2020 as the original goal for publishing this book, and then chose the date 05-05-2020 when the first goal wasn't met. 😊

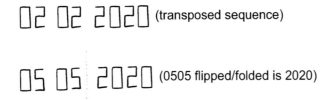

"What-do-YOU-see?"

Take a close look at the cover of this book. Do you see overlapping red and white <u>chicken wire</u>? <u>Cubes</u>? Do you see it as <u>flat/2D</u>? If you see it as <u>3D</u>, does it sink into the cover or pop out toward you?

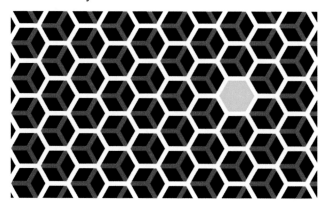

Below are some things seen by a few others. What do YOU see?

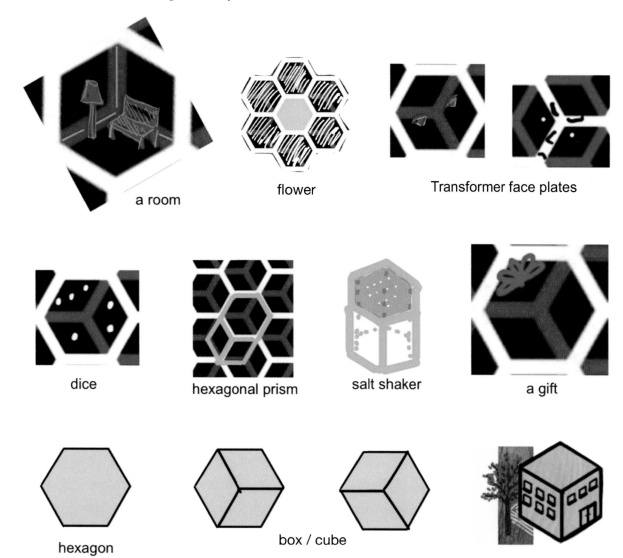

a room

flower

Transformer face plates

dice

hexagonal prism

salt shaker

a gift

hexagon

box / cube

125

Zag, Then Zig

In an attempt to show a student that each letter of the alphabet was just a symbol created to represent a spoken sound, I decided that we could create a few symbols of our own for some non-language sounds.

To represent a knock-once-on-the-desk sound, the student created a sort of lightning bolt shape with several zig zags. §§§ = knock

To represent a *clap*, I created a spiral symbol.

◎ = clap

We created a few other sound symbols and had fun drawing a few symbols in a row for the other person to decode. This was a good exercise for the student in order to better understand the connection between letters and sounds, but doing the activity also made me realize how hard it is to notice teeny differences in symbol formation. For example, we each recognized the other's symbols for "knocks" and "claps", but half the time, we drew them backwards! I drew his knock symbol starting like a Z (with a pencil stroke to the right), but he had designed it so that it started with a pencil stroke going to the left.

What if a spiral that started in the center and went outward in a clockwise direction represented a different sound than a spiral that started in the center but went outward in a counterclockwise manner? Does that remind you of any shapes in our alphabet?

Check out these Armenian symbols/letters from a candy tin. Seems confusing!

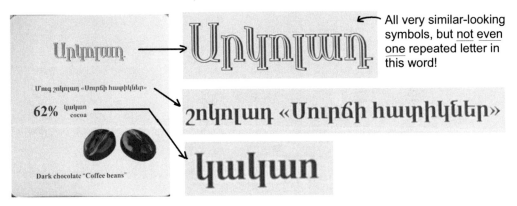

All very similar-looking symbols, but not even one repeated letter in this word!

We have similar-looking letters in our alphabet, too. The brain is amazing, though, and it can learn to decipher even the trickiest of symbols. But some brains must be shown how to turn off the "object viewing" skill when reading text and realize that the orientation and order of each symbol now matters.

APPENDIX C – Top Experts and Resources

New experts emerge, new articles and books are written, new videos and podcasts are created, and new assistive apps are developed every day. Some great resources will not be included here, but I have listed the ones that are the tippy top of my recommendation list. A look into any of these will likely lead you to other fantastic resources. Searching names or titles online is an option, but if you'd like a digital copy of these resources (so you can click directly on links), go to rcdyslexiacare.com or contact rcdyslexiacare@gmail.com to have one emailed to you.

Top People and their Articles / Books / Podcasts

Emily Hanford - senior education correspondent at APM Reports

Hard Words: Why Aren't Our Kids Being Taught to Read? Scientific research has shown how children learn to read and how they should be taught. (podcast/documentary)

At a Loss for Words: What's wrong with how schools teach reading (podcast/documentary)

Sally Shaywitz. M.D.

Overcoming Dyslexia (book)

Yale Center for Dyslexia and Creativity (organization)

Susan Barton

Bright Solutions for Dyslexia resources, guidance, research, videos, (website),

Dyslexia: Symptoms and Solutions (video)

Developer of the Barton Reading & Spelling System®, an Orton-Gillingham influenced approach that is multi-sensory, direct, explicit, structured and sequential (curriculum)

Seven essential phonemic awareness skills (list)

Ben Foss

The Dyslexia Empowerment Plan: A Blueprint for Renewing Your Child's Confidence and Love of Learning (book)

Headstrong Nation (organization)

"Ear Reading" - phrase coined by Ben Foss to describe listening to audio books

Be an Empowered Dyslexic (video)

Choose Strength, Not Shame (Ted Talk video)

Dr. Stanislas Dehaene – French cognitive scientist

Reading in the Brain: The New Science of How We Read (book)

How the Brain Learns to Read mirror generalization info at about 9 minutes (video)

Best way to teach reading (video)

David Kilpatrick, PhD

Why Phonemic Proficiency is Necessary Dr. Kilpatrick gives good information about how phonemic awareness proficiency leads to orthographic mapping, which leads to better word remembering, which leads to reading fluency (video)

Reading League Event Understanding Reading Development and Difficulties (video)

Essentials of Assessing, Preventing, and Overcoming Reading Difficulties (book)

Equipped for Reading Success - A comprehensive, step-by-step program of one-minute activities for developing phonemic awareness and fluent word recognition (program)

Brock Eide, M.D. M.A. and Fernadette Eide, M.D.

The Dyslexic Advantage: Unlocking the Hidden Potential of the Dyslexic Brain (book)

The Dyslexic Advantage (organization, website, dyslexia test)

Cliff Weitzman - college graduate and inventor of Speechify

Speechify (text to speech app)

Cliff explains that since he could not read, he would pretend to read at school by moving his finger and looking at a book. He would leave to go to the bathroom during reading circles. He loved when his Dad would read to him from the Harry Potter series, which led to him creating an app that will read aloud any text. (video)

Louisa Moats, Ed.D

How spelling supports reading: And why it is more regular and predictable than you think. *American Educator,*12-22, 42-43. (Winter 2005/06). (article)

Whole Language High Jinks. (2007). Washington, DC: Thomas Fordham Foundation. (article)

Whole language lives on: The illusion of "balanced" reading instruction. Moats, L.C. (2000). Washington, DC: Thomas Fordham Foundation. (article)

Teaching reading is rocket science (1999) Washington, DC: American Federation of Teachers. (article)

LETRS (Language Essentials for Teachers of Reading and Spelling) - LETRS® is a professional development series of books, workshops, and on-line courses for K-12 instruction in reading, spelling, and related language skills.

Dr. Steven Dykstra

Psychologist and well-known contributor on SpellTalk (a discussion group for researchers, educators, and other professionals dedicated to improving literacy. (free listserv)

Nancy Young

Ladder of Reading graphic that shows that Structured Literacy helps all students

Jamie Martin - assistive technology specialist

Assistive Technology guidance and recommendations

Mike Rowe
>   Mike Rowe Works - Foundation that recognizes that a good education doesn't always require a four-year degree. Work Ethic Scholarships encourage hard work and learning a high-demand skill. (organization, foundation)

Pam and Pete Wright
>   Wrightslaw - accurate, reliable information about special education law, education law, and advocacy (website)
>   From Emotions to Advocacy (book)

John Corcoran – The Teacher Who Couldn't Read
>   The Bridge to Literacy: No Child—or Adult—Left Behind (book)
>   The Teacher Who Couldn't Read: One Man's Triumph Over Illiteracy (book)
>   John Corcoran Foundation (organization, website, foundation)

Alison Clarke – Australian speech pathologist
>   Spelfabet (website, videos, resources)

Maryanne Wolf - Cognitive neuroscientist
>   Scholar, a teacher, and an advocate for children and literacy around the world

Charles Schwan and Beatrice McGarvey
>   Inevitable: Mass Customized Learning (book)

Joseph Torgesen
>   Catch Them Before They Fall (article)

Karin Merkle – Me! ☺
>   Rapid City Dyslexia Care (website)
>   Dyslexia presentation and panel of 7 people with dyslexia (DVD)
>   Razor the Resolute – Ultimate encourager and mascot of all-things-dyslexia
>   *Good News about Bright Children Who Struggle with Reading and Spelling* (article)
>   Now You See It: The Heart of Dyslexia (book)

Instruction and Curriculum supplemental to structured literacy

Foundation in Sounds

A pre-reading program that improves memory, discrimination, and sequencing of sounds, which are skills needed before starting structured literacy instruction (curriculum)

Institutes for Excellence in Writing

Written expression (curriculum)

Handwriting Without Tears
Strategies and materials to teach pencil grip, letter formation, and literacy skills needed for print and cursive handwriting (curriculum)

Times Tales DVD
Learning the most difficult to memorize times tables/multiplication facts (DVD)

Equipped for Reading Success
A comprehensive, step-by-step program of one-minute activities for developing phonemic awareness and fluent word recognition

Equipping Minds
Cognitive training that helps to improve executive functioning skills, working memory, and processing speed

Movies, Documentaries, and Videos about Dyslexia
The Big Picture: Rethinking Dyslexia
Embracing Dyslexia
Dyslexia: Symptoms and Solutions
Dislecksia, The Movie
Headstrong
Our Dyslexic Children

A few amazing people with dyslexia:
Ameer Baraka – actor

Patricia Polacco – children's book author and illustrator

"I wasn't a very good student in elementary school, and had a hard time with reading and writing. I didn't learn to read until I was almost 14 years old. Reading out loud for me was a nightmare because I would mispronounce words or reconstruct things that weren't even there. That's when one of my teachers discovered I had dyslexia. Once I got help, I read very well!"

"I came from a family of incredible storytellers, but I didn't start writing children's books until I was 41 years old. Drawing, painting, and sculpture have always been a part of my life, though. My family always encouraged my drawing ability. Kids in school who teased me about my reading would get out of their seats and stand behind my desk as I worked and go, "Wow, you can really draw." Later, I earned a degree in Fine Art, and got a Ph.D. in Art History."

Steven Spielberg - film director, producer, and screenwriter.

Willard Wigan – micro-sculptor (Look him up! You'll be amazed!)

Henry Winkler – actor and director, children's book author

Lindsey Stirling – electric violinist

Richard Branson – entrepreneur and philanthropist

> About the medical definition of dyslexia, Richard commented, "It's a bit like classifying someone who is left-handed as disabled because everyone else is right-handed, then teaching them to be right-handed, then pointing to a problem with coordination proving that there are disabled."

Charles Schwab - founder, chairman and CEO of Charles Schwab Corporation

Other:

Sink or Swim Appearance of Reading (article from a Kindergarten teacher about her realization of the need to examine how we teach reading)

Reading Rockets: Launching Young Readers (project, website) –
This national multimedia project offers interviews, a video series, and other resources designed to assist parents, teachers, and other educators in helping struggling readers build fluency, vocabulary, and comprehension skills.

Children of the Code (organization, website)
This non-profit organization has interviewed over 120 leaders in the fields of neuroscience, cognitive psychology, linguistics, orthography, instructional design, child, adult, and family literacy, teaching, government policy, and many other fields related to understanding the code and the challenges involved in learning to read it.

Thank you, Mr. Falker – Patricia Polacco's story about her own dyslexia, read by Jane Kaczmarek

Etymology / word origin (website)

The following two links are not related to dyslexia other than they demonstrate that it's easy to miss something you're not looking for, even when it's right in front of your nose, and then how hard it is to NOT see it once it's pointed out to you. Many teachers have not had dyslexia explicitly pointed out to them, so it's almost as if they are blind to dyslexia. Some students have not had language decoding explicitly pointed out to them, so it's almost as if they are blind to the details of words.

- Count the players (video)
- What is in the brick wall? (image and article)